Harry Barker – A Football Legend

Ed Lee

ISBN 978-1-4452-3966-8

Acknowledgements:

"The Triumph and Tragedy of Brazil's Forgotten Footballing Hero" by Ruy Castro

"How Pickles the dog dug up the accursed World Cup" by Paul Fleckney

http://www.mightyleeds.co.uk/ - author unknown.

For Bob

Introduction

This volume contains a record of footballer Harry Barker's personal history as dictated late in Harry's life to his biographer. Harry owns-up to being dishonest but how much he lies or embellishes the truth is something which only you, the reader, can decide. With the onset of old age and finding himself frequently having partaken excessively of the free alcohol available in the Football Association's Headquarters it may not be clear if these are the ramblings of a man who can no longer tell the difference between reality and his own vivid imagination, or if Harry is truly one of the most influential people of his generation.

In some respects Harry's memory proves to be very accurate. He is invariably correct in his recollection of match scores and the results of various football campaigns however there is no mention of Harry in any football club's history. Harry claims to have met several famous people, both from within and outside the football world. There is no corroboratory evidence to back up Harry's assertions and allegations and therefore we must assume that this biography is a work of fiction and that none of the events described herein actually occurred.

The biographer has attempted to record Harry's words as accurately as possible however Harry's inebriate state may have introduced some inaccuracies, in particular with the timing of events. For that the biographer apologises and hopes the reader will accept Harry's story for what it most likely is – an old man's fantasy.

Incidentally, as Harry dictated this record to the biographer he used the terms "Centre-Half" and "Centre-Back" inconsistently throughout. For the sake of clarity the biographer has settled on the term "Centre-Back". The biographer, in whose opinion the term "Centre-Half" became inapplicable once the central defenders dropped into line with the full-backs, hopes this does not offend the sensibilities of football aficionados. There are plenty of other matters in Harry's story which are bound to be considered far more offensive.

Contents

Early Years

Did all babies look like Winston Churchill, even before the war?

That's the thing about babies. Unless one's yours you can't really tell them apart. But, looking at the chubby face in this war-time photograph, it's obvious that I was special. Even so, nobody could have guessed that I would have gone on to become one of the most influential sportsmen of my generation - but I did. Yes, I made a career out of football and now, as I sit in the panelled rooms of the Football Association headquarters and look back on my rise to the upper echelons of the game, I can but marvel at the amount of good fortune that I have had, the famous people that I have met and influenced, the celebrated and notorious occasions that I have been part of and, of course, the women whose company I have enjoyed. And that's why I have decided to tell my story, just to prove to people that with the right attitude anything can be achieved.

Now when I say the right attitude I'm not talking about the "right" attitude that a school teacher or your priest might try to convince you is the route to triumph in life. You know "work hard", "give of your best", "play fair by other people and they'll play fair by you" and all that rubbish. What I'm talking about is keeping an eye for the main chance, doing the other fellow down and grabbing with both hands whatever bit of good fortune comes your way. And if somebody gets between you and what you want then you tread over them to get it. This is the real world I am talking about not some fairy tale where some nancy-looking Prince Charming steps in to prove that love conquers all, it don't, well not as promptly as a quick kick to the groin anyway. If the meek are going to inherit the earth then that means the rest of us are going to have to die first – so let's enjoy ourselves while we're here. As I look back over the last seventy years I can say, in a rare display of honesty mark you, that I have always done the right thing – for me at least. Why don't you be the judge of that?

Now one thing that I have not done much is to bear a grudge. If somebody has pushed ahead of me or snatched the last crumpet just as I was reaching for it then - fair enough. I wouldn't blame him because I'd do the same thing myself and I wouldn't waste my time fretting about getting even either. It ain't worth putting the effort into getting an eye for your eye 'cos what would happen if you were to lose your other eye trying to get even? Exactly! But this isn't a book about philosophy or morality, it's about football, and believe me morality don't come into it. Mind you, if the chance comes along to give someone a payback then I say always take it, particularly if they don't know it is you that did for 'em and especially if you can shift the blame onto someone else. In many ways life is like a game of football. If somebody kicks your ankle then it's your given right to hack them down. If it's from behind and the referee doesn't see you then that's all the better.

This photo that I now hold in my wrinkled hand predates any of my memories. I found it amongst my Mother's things and I don't recognise the fellow holding me. It's certainly not Dad. It's an American airman and written on the back is the word "Chuck". So either my Mother was going to throw this out or his name is Charles and I'd bet this is the Charles Mulligan whose existence came to light many years ago at a very opportune moment. I can tell he is a big fellow because, like me, he has to bow his head in order to fit into the doorway of Mum's house. Amongst Mum's things there is another photograph of him, a bit older, all padded up like one of those American Footballers. Although why they call that football I don't know. They're always picking up the ball with their hands and none of them can kick a ball anything other than a long way in a straight line - just like me really.

Mum lived in that terraced house for most of her life. It was the kind of place that looked just as depressing in black and white as it was in colour. We had two bedrooms upstairs and a parlour and "front room" downstairs. It was plenty for us and somehow we got by when we had visitors. Even during the war Mum stayed in that house in Leeds. Dad was away in the army of course. I understand he had a distinguished career in His Majesty's Armed Services and returned to us, albeit briefly, in one piece. He told me "Harry, my father, Granddad Barker" (who served in the Great War) "said 'always look after your feet'. So I did, and whenever there was trouble I made sure my feet were looked after and pointing in the right direction – away from it". Not a bad motto, that. I understand Granddad Barker ran off with a French dancer so it could be he picked up that bit of advice from her.

I think I remember Dad coming home at the end of the war when I was about three – but I could be confused about that because Dad was often away for long periods. Six months here and a year there. But when he was at home he'd always come to watch me playing football. That was the one thing that Dad and I did together. I can't remember much about my early childhood or the rest of our family but I do remember that several of my uncles were footballers. Mum would often meet them when they were playing in Leeds and bring them home on a Friday night so that on a Saturday morning they could take me early to the ground and get me a good place to stand. I'd often get the chance to warm up with the players and they'd try to teach me some of their skills, but it was no good. The only thing I managed to do was to hit the ball hard. All that Fancy-Dan stuff with cutting inside or using the outside of your foot to curl a ball… what's that all about? Hard and long, that's my motto and it has served me well.

As Dad was away quite a lot my uncles would often stay in the house overnight to keep me and Mum company. They'd usually bring something with them like a leg of lamb or a tripe or even, once, a steak. I remember that well, particularly the blood dripping onto the floor. Not from the steak you understand - but I'd tried to snatch the larger portion and Mum had fetched me a wallop across my face that had made my head ring and my nose bleed. Mum always made sure I got a good share though. She ran a tight, disciplined household and I learned very early who was the boss at home.

I also remember the bars of chocolate. Food was rationed long after the war but I never went without. So while the other kids in our street looked like sticks of celery I grew bigger, some would say fatter, and taller. So much so that by the time our teacher at St Runwald's school, Mr McKee, picked a school team there was only one possible choice for the centre of midfield, yours truly. There I was, six inches (what's that? 15 centimetres – whatever they are) taller than the next boy and a good two stone heavier. Don't ask me what that is in the metric system just believe me – when I ran at the opposition defence they had two choices – get out of the way or get trampled. Once I was within range of the goal I would just let fly and if the goal-keeper was silly enough to get in the way then more fool him. They soon learned.

So, by the age of nine, I was recognised as the most lethal footballer in the district. Over a hundred goals in my first season and it wasn't hard. Some of the parents didn't like it. They didn't think it was "fair". Whatever that means! Apparently some of them wanted me to play rugby instead. They must be joking – have you seen that game? Somebody could get hurt!

I'll tell you what wasn't fair though. It was shortly after my tenth birthday. I remember it well because I'd had a bit of a bad day myself. As usual at afternoon break I'd taken a ball to the back of the school canteen to practise my shooting. I was alone as I had failed to find somebody to press into being in goal. For some reason the other boys were not keen on standing in the "goal" while I powered shots at them from close range. The round swill-bin, being about a yard (metre?) high and about two foot wide (you know what a foot is, don't you?) made an excellent goal-post. The other goal post was made by the black drain-pipe which ran from the drain cover up to the roof of the school.

These were the post-war days when schools provided "proper" food for all their pupils, notoriously labelled "school dinners". These meals were compulsory which meant that on this day every member of the school, teachers included, had been faced with a portion of beef stew, nearly-mashed potatoes and watery, tasteless carrots which, I promise you, had been boiled for at least a fortnight to ensure that all traces of flavour had been removed. It therefore followed that, as an edible item, the carrots were at an advantage over the rest of the meal and most of them had been eaten. The stew however was quite revolting, the little meat was gristly and some pupils were seen chewing single chunks for minutes until their jaws ached and they had to return it, unsubtly and accompanied by a volume of drool from their mouths to their plates. The gravy was bland but some was eaten to moisten the less solid bits of potato. This day the revolting stew had led to revolt and eventually most of it was consigned to the swill-bin. You may be unfamiliar with the swill-bin. Nothing was wasted in those days so the uneaten food from our school was put into the swill-bin and left at the rear of the canteen for collection by a local pig-farmer. He'd feed it to his pigs. Who, no doubt, at some time, would themselves provide meat for an equally inedible school meal. I guess that's what passed for re-cycling in those days.

So I stood ten yards away from my makeshift target just inside the high wire fence, which both protected the local resident's gardens from our excesses and imprisoned us for seven hours every school-day, and blasted the ball against the wall of the canteen. I could do this for hours. Every shot a cracker. The goalie, had there been one, would have no chance. And then a mistake! I was just taking a shot to win the F.A Cup for Leeds when the ball crashed against the inside of the post. The swill-bin lifted on its edge and balanced for a moment as it decided whether to topple over or right itself. After due consideration the choice was made and it turned over with a dull clank. The ghastly stew spilled out, spreading like lumpy paint across the asphalt. Without hesitation I collected the ball and scarpered leaving the brown mess to seep further and further over the impermeable ground.

There was a match after school that day and once again we thrashed our nameless visitors. A couple of their players left the field crying after I had bundled them to the ground (I found it always worth adding a little kick as the players fell – it isn't difficult to make it look like an accident and I find it encourages them to get out of the way next time.) As usual I'd scored all the goals and I remember one parent calling out "Why don't you let somebody else score for a change?" Now why would I want to do that?

After the game Mr McKee asked to speak to Mum and me. Mr McKee was a Scot by the way but he still liked to win football matches so I imagine he wasn't completely happy about the situation that he found himself. He also must have known that Mum wouldn't be best pleased so, knowing her reputation, he made sure that he spoke to us in front of all the other parents. He told Mum that the other schools were refusing to play St Runwald's at football because too many of the boys were getting hurt in the games and that because of my skill and strength (no, he really said that) the games weren't competitive.

Now I was a bit confused by all this but Mum seemed to grasp what he was saying immediately. I knew something was wrong pretty soon though because Mum, who was quite tall and deceptively strong, grabbed Mr McKee by the throat with her right hand. I knew how strong that right hand was because I had felt it across my back-side on quite a few occasions. Mr McKee was no weakling but the pure aggression emanating from my Mother seemed to shock him into inaction. She then began to push him backwards and to speak very closely into his face. Flecks of spit appeared on his cheeks while drops of sweat trickled from his forehead to meet them. He seemed to be croaking out an explanation that there was nothing he could do about it all. It was the Headmistress's decision. Mum was having none of it. "I thought you picked the team" she cried "are you going to let some woman dictate to you who plays in your own football team?" She suddenly released Mr McKee who, unsupported, fell backwards into the muddy goal area. Mum looked down imperiously on him as he squirmed in the mud and asked the unanswerable questions. "Why don't you stand up for yourself? What are you a man or a mouse?"

To Mr McKee's relief Mum turned and strode away. Taking my hand she said "We'll talk to your father about this". This was my cue to start crying. I didn't mind blubbing in front of my team-mates because I'd seen most of them in tears. I was usually the cause, after all. I never have worried about shedding a tear for effect and these days in football it seems the losing team's dressing rooms are awash with salt water week in, week out. I suppose, like me, they think that if the Boss sees them crying he'll reckon they're really upset at losing and so "committed to the cause" that there'd be no point giving them a hard time. My logic was similar. If Dad was getting involved then somebody was going to get a good hiding so if I'm crying already then that puts me in the clear and he'd look for somebody else. This time that "somebody else" was going to be poor Mr McKee.

Once Mum told Dad they were dropping me from the team he was after Mr McKee like a particularly well-trained greyhound after a plump rabbit. Mr McKee had just got up and was trying to brush some of the mud from his tweed jacket when he heard, or probably felt the vibrations of, Dad approaching. "Oi! You!" called Dad. Mr McKee turned and saw this tank-like man approaching. Dad wasn't tall, he was much shorter than Mum and only a few inches taller than I was at the time, but Dad was "Big". He had arms like legs as they say and the rounded shoulders of a hard labourer, which is what he was. He could move too and as Mr McKee broke into a run so did Dad. I was quite surprised. Mr McKee didn't look that quick but when he turned the corner of the school playground he had left Dad twenty yards further behind. It was no good though. There was no escape around that corner as it led into the enclosed playground behind the canteen. I think I heard Mr McKee crash into the wire-netting. Whenever I see footage on TV of a wild animal throwing itself against a fence franticly, but futilely, trying to escape from a predator I think of Mr McKee on that day. There appeared to be no escape from Dad. However this time fortune favoured the cowardly and as Dad turned the corner fully intent on his pursuit he failed to notice the greasy puddle which had spread across his path. The thick stew had congealed to form a putrid slick and Dad's right foot hit it at pace. As his right leg slipped to the side his left leg landed heavily on his right ankle and Dad fell to the ground with a resounding curse. Mr McKee saw his chance and hurtled back onto the playing fields his stride lengthening like a champion long-distance runner approaching the tape. Dad rose and hobbled after him, covered from the waist down in the nauseating goo.

Mum and I left him to it. I kept crying until we were off the playing fields by which time I thought it safe to stop. Dad came home late that night. He'd probably stopped off on the way home for a "quick one" so I heard him singing as he fumbled his key into the door-lock. Early the next morning some policemen came to speak to Dad, something about parole conditions, and it was another trip away for him.

Back at school a rosy-faced Mr McKee was being treated as a hero and a few weeks later it was announced that there would be no football teams at the school. The Headmistress had decided that cricket was a sport that would develop the boys' sporting instincts better. And she was right or course. I mean there's no crying and cheating in cricket is there?

All this didn't matter to me because Mum had received a letter. The District School's Football Committee had invited me to trial for their team and that was to be the next step forward in my trip to the stars.

Youth Club Football

Now I suppose this book represents my memoirs so we ought to cover some basic facts. I, Harold Thomas Barker OBE, was born on October 9th 1942 in St James Hospital, Leeds. Even that hospital became famous as "Jimmy's" in its own seven year TV series in the late 80's but not ONCE did they mention that I had been born there and I sat through every bloody episode waiting for a mention. My Mother's name was Elizabeth Mary Patricia Barker née O'Shaughnessy – so I could have played for Ireland if Jack Charlton had wanted a 50 year old. Dad was Owen Thomas Reuben Barker, known to most people as "Tom". Don't ask about the "Reuben" – I suspect that my grandfather had made a deal with the doctor to get something knocked off the bill.

As I said, I went to St Runwald's School, Leeds until the age of eleven and then onto Parkmore Secondary School. But at that point my non-footballing education became irrelevant which was lucky because I was no scholar. The good thing about Parkmore was that it was near the town centre. That meant that I could bunk-off and disappear into the cinema, or wherever, quite quickly. It was a mixed school - so there were girls - and I was popular amongst the girls, more-so than amongst the other boys. I don't think they liked me but there I was: blond-haired, broad-shouldered and well over six foot at the age of fifteen. I stood out, and the girls liked that. I liked it too. There's no point being backward in coming forward and I wasn't. The school held nothing for me – other than the girls.

Another reason I was popular was that as I was spending more and more time training and playing football. I was fit. The fat of my early years had disappeared. Of course I had been picked for the District Team and from there local youth teams were queuing up to sign me. I had converted from mid-field to become a centre-back by then. Not a difficult job really. You hang around at the back and the first time their nippy forwards come near you they get a good hard wallop. After that they're not so keen and I can just clean up by hitting the ball long and hard up the field. Of course that means I don't get to score too many goals but then I'd scored more than enough in my time and even scoring goals had lost some of its fascination. At fifteen there were other things on my mind. Girls.

Now if my Mother had taught me one thing it was to treat women with respect. I'd seen her flatten a couple of fellows who'd made the mistake of thinking she was something other than a lady. So the golden rule given to me by Mum was to be a gentleman, and Mum was right. It works, well ninety-nine times out of a hundred, anyway.

Football tends to attract the pretty girls and at the end of my first season with Park Lane Youth Football Club there were no problems getting a date. The problem was getting the right date. The centre-forward at the club was a lad called Stan Shadwell. He went on to have a bit of a career in football but in those days he was a short, slim, weedy fellow; always well-dressed, the sort of fellow that would look good even in a sack. And worse, the girls loved him, especially Rose Levington.

Now Rose was a beauty. At least 5' 10" tall she was just the right height for me. She and short-arse had been going out for ages, at least three months, which was ten weeks longer than I'd ever kept a girl-friend. Tall and slim with straight dark-brown hair and the smoothest complexion outside a bowl of cream she was the best looking girl in the whole of Leeds and I was brought up to believe that I deserved nothing but the best. We'd shared a joke and a laugh together on a few occasions but Stan was always hovering nearby, ready to shepherd her away before I could make a move.

Stan was the glamour boy at the club. With two games to go he had scored far more goals than any other player in the league that season and would clearly win the golden-boot. I put it around that it was only because he hadn't come up against a centre-back like me that he'd scored so many goals but the reality was that even in training he could go past me as if I wasn't there. I couldn't kick him if I couldn't catch him. The other forwards in the league were not so lucky.

The team had done well that season and were likely to win the league championship. A small thing now but when you're fifteen these things seem to matter, to some people at least. The biggest problem on my mind, however, was how to prise Rose away from Stan and it would be some good payback for my regular humiliation in training if I could do that in time for the annual presentation dance. We had a home fixture against our main rivals, Pottery YFC, and a win would seal the title. It was during that game that I came up with a plan. Unfortunately my moment of inspiration coincided with a Pottery attack and before I knew it I was chasing their centre-forward back towards our goal having given him a five yard start. I was quick over a straight-line distance but even I couldn't catch him to stop him poking the ball into the bottom corner of our goal. Like all good defenders I followed through putting my studs into the back of his calves then I jumped up to allow his team-mates to compound his injury as they leapt on top of him in celebration. He wouldn't be moving so quickly for a week or so. Of course I then turned to our left full-back and berated him for not covering the run. Here's the first rule of survival in football - always blame somebody else when you've made a mistake on the pitch. Get your criticism in first.

Going one down was a disappointment but in a way it helped with my scheme. We were, of course, desperate to equalise. A loss would mean Pottery would need just a win in their last game to take the title. Late in the second half I saw my chance. We'd won a corner and although usually (because of my natural speed and the fact that I could never be bothered to sprint back to our own half after a corner was taken) I would cover anybody they left up the pitch by standing around the centre-spot allowing everybody else to take their place in the opposition penalty area. This time I said to the aforementioned full-back "Oi! Useless! You've done enough damage today now you stay back here while I go forward and try to rescue something out of this game." He tried to protest but I ignored him and jogged forward marking my target.

I timed my run perfectly. The corner was lumped in. With the heavy leather ball of the day it was impossible to do much more than pump it into the box. It was met at the near-post by their defender but his headed clearance was not strong enough and the ball fell to the feet of none other than dear Stan Shadwell. This was my chance. I had gathered momentum as I approached the goal. A big Pottery defender was trying to reach Stan but I would get there first. As I neared I rose and flew in, both feet first, studs up, and made full-contact with Stan's standing foot. I heard the crack. The Pottery defender arrived a fraction of a second later as Stan screamed and fell. The ball trickled away and the referee had no hesitation. He awarded us a penalty and sent the Pottery defender off.

Now this is when it pays to obey the second rule of football. Keep your wits about you at all times. Of course the Pottery defender proclaimed his innocence, he would though wouldn't he? But the evidence was incontrovertible. Stan probably had a broken leg. Who else could have done it? Certainly not the tall, blond, broad-shouldered and obviously shocked Park Lane player who had already grabbed the match-ball in anticipation of taking the penalty – you see unfortunately the team's usual penalty taker had recently suffered an injury and was being carried, unceremoniously, off the pitch. So the opportunity for glory was there for the taking.

It wasn't the best directed penalty that has ever been taken but after all those hours practising behind the canteen at school I was confident, and if the goalie had managed to get a finger to it as it rocketed into the back of the net then it would probably have ripped the digit off. As the man of the moment I accepted the plaudits, even from the full-back who had dared to come up the pitch to join the celebrations. Of course I reminded him that I expected him to concentrate for the rest of the game and he said "Yes, sorry about earlier." "No problem," I replied "I know you can play better". "Thanks" he said and we were all friends again.

Both sides were now down to ten men. There were no substitutes in those days and the match ended at one all. That was good enough for us as the following week we comfortably won our last game against poor opposition and were crowned Champions. That wasn't too important to me. The important thing was that Rose didn't have a date for the end of season dance, yet!

It wasn't as difficult as I thought to get Rose to the dance. She desperately wanted to go. You see in those days there were no "Discos" and "Clubs" open every night of the week and when a dance came along everybody wanted to be there. Of course Rose would have any number of lads desperate to take her so my timing was important. I "happened" to bump into her on the way to school on the Monday. It was actually my last week there. Yes, in that civilised world we were allowed to leave school at fifteen rather than enduring further years of torture, not just for those of us who didn't want to be incarcerated daily but also for the swots who did want to be there but didn't want us bullying them during the course of their educational day.

Of course I asked how Stan was and Rose explained she'd been to the hospital to visit him on the Sunday evening after the game. Stan was claiming that it was me who had broken his leg and that it had been deliberate. I feigned shock at this accusation. I was terribly upset. How could he possibly say that? Everybody saw the opposition defender charge in – that was why he was sent off. Why, if I had broken somebody's leg I'd never play football again. Rose was very sympathetic so I thought the time was right to push home my advantage.

"Look, Rose." I said "Now Stan is in hospital you won't have anybody to go to the dance with. I feel really bad about him being injured, especially as he is blaming me. How about if I were to take you to the dance myself, you know, just as friends? I am sure Stan wouldn't mind. He'd probably be happy that his injury isn't stopping you from going."

She wasn't convinced so I played the ace which I had just been dealt.

"Of course, if you believe that I hurt Stan on purpose then I'd understand."

"No, no, no." She answered "Of course I don't blame you. I'd be happy to go to the dance with you and I'm sure Stan will understand".

She may be sure but I was absolutely bloody certain he'd understand and that he'd be livid. And I was right. When Rose visited him in hospital later in the week he had been so infuriated to learn that she was going to the dance with me that he'd tried to get out of bed. He'd put his bone out again and set his recovery back another fortnight. Perhaps the pain caused him to lose his temper and when he'd finished telling Rose what he thought of her (I think the word "Jezebel" came into it somewhere) the poor girl was so upset that she chucked him in there and then. And where do you think she found a suitably broad shoulder to cry on?

Trials and Tribulations

The end of season dance went well and my romance with Rose began to take its brief but pleasant course. We had fun, but not as much fun as I had dreamt of. I recall that sometimes those dreams were very real with embarrassing results but let's get back to my football career.

Being a championship winning team also meant that club scouts would come to check out the talent. With Stan sidelined for the first half of the next season there wasn't much to look at but they still came from clubs all over the North. You see travelling to Leeds meant an overnight stay and an overnight stay meant a hotel, a meal, a good drink and some interesting company so the scouts were keen to keep Leeds on their itinerary. When they put their expenses in they had to justify their trip so they needed to report on good local talent – the professional clubs don't want to read that a scout has spent £5 on a trip to Leeds only to report that they saw nobody worth signing so, as Stan was no longer in contention, good reports were sent back to the clubs with the conclusion "monitor progress" against my name.

Unfortunately they were looking for players with a bit more ability than I had. In those days being big, strong and quick wasn't enough to get you into a professional football club. Fortunately that would change. Mum, however, wanted nothing but the best for me. She had realised some years ago that I was not University material and that my best chance of making a bare living outside the factory gates was in football. She said sport was in my blood, but the only sport Dad understood was the "Sport of Kings". Yes, he understood that pretty well. He could lose more money in one hour in the bookies than most people could earn in a fortnight but he believed you had to stick at things so he never gave up. Come to think of it I think that the only place in Leeds that Dad was popular and welcomed <u>was</u> the bookies. They always seemed to be smiling when he walked in. So I suppose Mum meant my sporting instincts came through her family line.

So the scouts came to watch. Now, as I mentioned before, Mum seemed to know a lot of footballers. Mum would come to watch me play on Sundays and would meet people that she had known, presumably through my uncles, from the footballing world. There was one particular man that Mum brought home and introduced as Uncle Alex. I am not sure which branch of the family he was from because he had a very strong Glaswegian accent. So much so that I couldn't actually understand much of what he said. Perhaps there was a link through the Irish part of our family. He seemed to get on well with Mum though and Mum seemed to like him as she told me to pay attention to him as he was going to "see me right". One Saturday morning I overheard raised voices in the parlour. I stood outside the door and listened as Alex whined "But Lizzie, the boy hasna' goat it. I canna' send him for a trial. They'll want tae knae what ah've been dain' here in Leeds".

"Aye." said Mum (that accent is contagious isn't it?) "And they're not the only ones. Your wife is going to want to know a bit more and my Tom is going to be out in three weeks time."

"But Lizzie, if I put him up for a trial I'll lose my job. I canna' dae it. I've nae choice."

"I'll give you a choice" said Mum "either I tell my Tom about you or I tell your wife. How's that for a choice?"

"Jayzus, Lizzie, have a heart. He'll kill me."

"And so will your wife but at least with my Tom it'll be quick. Now this is what I want. I want Harry to have his trial and I want him in that club."

"But Lizzie!"

"I want him in that club. He is going to have a career in football and if you know what's good for you then you'll do as I tell you."

I stood quietly outside the door and listened as Alex submitted. He'd do his best, and he did. Some may have felt embarrassed at their lack of talent being so openly discussed but I didn't. I knew I wasn't very good but I had already learned that ability didn't matter too much if you've got the desire; and I had the desire all right. Working five and a half days a week for a pittance in a noisy factory or a filthy mine didn't sound half as good as kicking a ball around for a couple of hours every Saturday afternoon. Footballers didn't earn much more than an ordinary working man in those days – but there were the bonuses. I'm not just talking about a few quid extra for a win. I'm talking about the money-making opportunities in the bookies and, of course, the birds. I mean like England Captain Billy Wright - he was walking out with one of the Beverley Sisters.

A couple of weeks later Mum received a letter from none other than Manchester United offering me a trial. We both acted surprised but I don't think either of us was very convincing.

Now that isn't the kind of thing that you keep to yourself so before the game on the Sunday morning I was at Park Lane YFC waving my letter in the face of all the other players and the manager. "Here," I said "take a look at this. I'm going to be off playing for a real club soon. I'm going to be the next John Charles and if you lot are lucky you may get to see me play." I laughed loudly. I thought I heard somebody whisper "Good, maybe he'll bugger off to Italy too" but I ignored it. This was my moment of triumph. I mean you've got to enjoy your victories haven't you?

Stan had come to watch the game. His leg was still in plaster and he was weeks away from resuming training. I made sure he got a good look at the letter by waving it provocatively under his nose. I then called out to Rose, surprisingly still my girlfriend at the time.

"Hey, Rose, shall we go out and have a special celebration tonight?" She smiled lightly. Thinking back I should have noticed the sympathetic look she gave Stan but, to be honest, I was a little full of myself at the time. Now you may think I was over-confident but then I had heard Mum's conversation with Uncle Alex and Mum always got what she wanted. Dad would be back soon and he usually saw to any problems. So with Mum, Dad and Uncle Alex on my side I knew I was in. Next stop Manchester United!

As it turned out my boorish behaviour worked to my advantage. I played my usual average game for Park Lane. I couldn't be bothered to kick anybody and at all costs wanted to avoid injury so, as soon as the ball came near me, I would punt it up-field. I lashed out onto one loose ball which dropped at the feet of our centre-forward in the penalty area and led to the only goal of the game so I reckon I did my bit. Of course my trial with Manchester United was all the talk at pitch-side where, as usual, three or four club scouts were loitering - pretending to watch the game whilst eyeing up the player's girlfriends and mothers. Once they heard that one of the players was going for trials with the biggest club in the country they paid a bit more attention. Understandable really. How could they go back to their clubs and tell them that they have missed out on a player who Manchester United saw fit to trial? By the end of the game all of the scouts had managed to speak to Mum and a few days later there were six more letters – word gets around – offering me trials at various clubs. Leeds had come in of course, so had Manchester City, West Bromwich Albion, Sheffield Wednesday, Sunderland and, seriously, Bradford Park Avenue!

I don't suppose many of you remember Bradford Park Avenue. At time of writing they are still about but even in 1958 they were languishing near the bottom of the old Third Division North. That was about as bad as it got for a League club so I wanted to throw their letter straight into the bin but Mum said I should go to all the trials offered. Bradford was just a short distance away so I guess there was no harm. It would mean a day out for me and Mum could visit the shops. She'd enjoy that. I should explain that although there was plenty of work around in Leeds at the time and I had left school some months ago I hadn't quite got round to finding myself a job. Mum kept a lot of cash around the house so money wasn't a problem.

I don't know where the money came from but we were never short of enough to get us by and to afford a bit more than life's essentials. We were the first people down our street to get a television and when I saw the advertisement for Stanley Matthews Football Boots I decided I should have a pair. All I had to do was to explain to Mum that they were all I needed to guarantee a place at Manchester United and she was off to the Co-op for a pair of size elevens. I looked forward to showing them to people and telling them we had seen them advertised on our T.V.

The "Avenue" trip was first. We travelled by train the following Thursday morning and got a taxi from the station to the stadium. When Mum told the cab driver that we'd like to go to Bradford Park Avenue Football Club he answered "Are you sure?" I think he was a City fan.

There aren't many cities now in England that have two league football clubs but in those days Bradford did. But, of course, only one could survive and it was a fight to the death. Bradford City would be the winners, going on to set a Premiership record of avoiding relegation having accumulated the fewest number of points. History does not record my part in that battle and although they didn't know it Thursday 14th November 1957 was a day of significance for "Park Avenue" and the events of which would, one day, change their fate.

Mum was never one to "mother" me and, as much as she would support my football career, if it was a choice between spending a few hours looking at clothes in the exclusive and exotic shops in Bradford City Centre or of watching me run around a bit of grass there was no contest. She'd be back by three o'clock.

I'd brought my new boots and Park Lane football kit in a small bag. I hadn't wanted to bring the new boots but Mum insisted. "You'll need to wear them in before the trial at Manchester United so this is an ideal opportunity" she said. So, full of confidence, and maybe a little contempt, I walked over to a man who had just ridden up on an ancient black bicycle. I looked down on him as he bent to take of his bicycle clips.

"Hey mate." I said "Do you know where I can find Mr Ripley?" The man lifted his head and asked "What do you want him fer?"

"I'm here for a trial."

"Oh! You are, are you? Then you'd better come with me" and he set off at a steady pace along the back of a rusty stand to a small wooden door.

He produced a key and as he opened the door I was met with the sight of a muddy football pitch with hardly a blade of grass on it. The pitch was surrounded by three rusting metal and concrete stands with just one area supplied with executive seating – that is to say some long wooden benches which had been fixed to the ground presumably to prevent their theft by the local railway should they be short of sleepers. It slipped out "Blimey, what a dump. It's hardly the Arsenal is it?" They say first impressions are often right.

It wasn't that I was wrong it's just that my timing was poor. As I spoke two young men turned the corner. "Hello, Mr Ripley." said the taller "What you got there?"

"He's here for a trial." replied my guide who I now realised was the man that I had come to see.

"What as? A goal-post?" The shorter of the men looked up at me but not as most people usually did. There was no fear in this little man's eyes. "Mind you, lad, if you think this place is a dump, maybe you're too good for us. We wouldn't want to take up any of your time if you don't think we're up to your mark."

I could see that this was likely to be the shortest trial ever so I thought I'd better say something but then Mr Ripley, who'd been sizing me up, cut in

"Now, now, Len. Don't be too hasty. The lad has come a long way so I think we should give him his chance."

There was a glint in his eye as he said this and the two players, because that's what they were, offered no contrary arguments. There was a wink and a chuckle which I took as encouragement for me. I was relieved that the trial was going ahead. I mean, Mum wasn't due back for at least another three hours and there was nothing else for me to do around here. What's more if she heard that I messed up the trial for the sake of a few words she'd take it out on me and even at 6 foot 4 I didn't fancy another wallop from Mum.

I was shown to a shabby but, to be fair, clean changing room where I put on my kit and boots. The boots were state of the art. Made from a strong brown leather which covered my foot over my ankle they included nailed in wooden studs and a reinforced leather cap over the toes which felt at tough as steel. I laced them up tight, right to the bottom of my shin. In time the boots would soften and mould to my foot. As you can imagine these solid boots protected the foot admirably; they were also lethal weapons in the wrong hands …. or on the wrong feet.

I went out onto the pitch just as it started to drizzle with rain. Mr Ripley and the two players were waiting for me. The players had changed and were wearing light running shoes.

"Ok." said Ripley "We'll start with some fitness. Len, why don't you trot the boy around the pitch a few times?"

"Come on, lad." called Len as he jogged at a fair pace along the near touchline. "Don't go on the grass, lad, we have to save the green for the games." I looked but try as I might I couldn't find a blade of grass to keep off.

Well, as we ran, Len gradually increased his pace, so much so that I'd fallen behind after the first lap. "Come on lad, keep up." called Ripley. So I lengthened my stride and got within touching distance of Len who kept running steadily. We completed two laps which was as much as I usually did in training but Len kept going. Maybe, I thought, the professional clubs do three times round. They are professionals after all. Well Len ran a fourth and then a fifth. My boots has started to rub after the first couple of hundred yards and after five laps my feet were becoming very painful as the leather rubbed through my woollen socks. The rain was now a steady torrent and I found myself splashing through puddles. My socks, shorts and shirt were soaked through and the muddy water flicked off the back of Len's feet to fly upwards into my face and up my nose. I should mention, for those unfamiliar with Yorkshire weather trends, that it isn't particularly warm most November afternoons in Bradford. In that, the weather on the day was typical. As we neared the end of the sixth lap I could see than Len was slowing down. Thank God for that, I thought. I slowed with him as he approached Ripley.

"What's wrong, Len?"

"It's my thigh" said Len "it's tightening up. I'm sorry I can't go on. I'll have to rest it."

I wished I that I had thought of that.

"Well that's no good." Ripley exclaimed "What about this lad's trial? He isn't warmed up properly yet!"

Catching my breath I gasped "I am. I am." but he didn't listen because then the other Charlie, whose name was Charlie as it happens, piped up.

"That's OK. I'll take him round."

"Good" said Ripley "off you go then" and as Charlie set off he gave me a brief word to inspire me "Go on lad, get after him. You're doing well so far".

So off I went chasing Charlie as Ripley and Len took cover under the shade of the rusty stand. I continued to splash along never managing to get within five yards of him. My lungs began to ache as I fought for breath. The rain poured down plastering my hair to my forehead then dripping into my eyes and onto my nose. The good news was that I didn't feel the pain in my chest or legs because the agony of my sore feet and raw ankles was all I could think about. I do not know how many laps Charlie and I ran but I could see that Charlie, whilst wet, was as fresh as a daisy when he was waved down by Ripley and Len.

"What's up?" asked Charlie.

"It's Len" said Ripley "his thigh is a lot better now so he needs to run to loosen it off. He can take over now".

"Fine." said Charlie and Len started running.

"Go on, lad. You're nearly done now. Just a little more then I reckon you'll be ready." Ripley waved me on my way like a benevolent grandfather.

So off I went again, my shorts and shirt stuck to my body and legs. My feet still in agony and the rain, well it rained! Each lap had become slower and slower. Len had clearly reduced his speed and kept looking over his shoulder to give me encouragement. You know, things like "put some effort in lad!" or "move you lazy sod!" but now I could hardly put one foot in front of the other and nearly slipped over in the mud. I looked down and noticed that my boots had collected about a pound of earth on each foot making each step that little bit harder.

"He's ready!" called Len cheerfully as he trotted into the shelter of the stand and I followed him in and collapsed onto the steps.

"Right." said Ripley "Now for some football. Will you go and get the balls?" He asked pointing to a sack at the side of the pitch.

"Balls?" I asked and lay out on the concrete.

Seeing I was all-in Ripley chuckled as he suggested we could finish the trial another day. "Maybe this club isn't for you, lad. It is, after all, a bit of a dump."

"Balls." I croaked.

Charlie offered to put the kettle on. And the three disappeared into a small office. I could hear them sniggering as I lay there cursing. Now I know I told you I don't believe in planning revenge, well I don't, but I put down a marker that if ever I got the chance to give them, or this club, some pay-back – then I would. Meanwhile the biggest thing on my mind was to find a way to get those sodden boots off!

United

Over the next few weeks the trials at Leeds, Manchester City, Sheffield Wednesday and Sunderland passed without incident. It was always pretty much the same routine. We'd arrive, get changed, there'd be a group of nervous lads trying to appear nonchalant and me, glaring at them all with a superior air. I felt it important to make sure they knew who the boss was, and if any of them looked a bit useful I took the time to explain to them that if they came anywhere near me on the pitch I would kick them so hard it'd be their last game of football, never mind a trial. It worked. They didn't want to get injured so I was clear to continue pumping the ball the length of the field whenever it came near me. Fortunately my feet had recovered from the Bradford incident. After a quick warm up – usually running – we'd have a short game then it was "Good-Bye lads. We'll be in touch." Perhaps they were very good judges of a player or it was guesswork based on the scouts reports. I suspect it was just guesswork or the old "who you know" syndrome - and my Mum knew a lot of people.

Dad was back so sometimes he would take Mum and me to the clubs. If he could borrow a car he would come but Dad didn't like travelling by train. I think he objected to buying a ticket and as Mum didn't want anything to go wrong on these trials she wouldn't let him come unless he bought one. But going to these trials was just an opportunity for me to practise and for Mum to have a day out. We all knew that Manchester United were the only team for me.

The trial at West Brom, or to give them their full title, West Bromwich Albion, was more significant because I met a relative who later became a business associate of mine. Dad didn't accompany us on that trip, which was a shame because the train journey across country to Birmingham was so long that we had to stay overnight. Mum met Uncle Vic at the ground so after the trial we all had a fish and chip supper then I went off to bed and left Mum and Uncle Vic in the bar so they could finished off the evening with a "quick one" - as Uncle Vic put it with a snigger. The following morning Mum said she was confident that I'd done well enough to be offered an apprenticeship at West Brom. Uncle Vic had popped back, still in the same suit and tie that he had worn the evening before, to say good-bye and get some breakfast. He said that it was the athleticism that clinched it. That surprised me because I didn't think I'd done a lot of running about. I only wanted United. Mum seemed to be blushing. I guess she was very proud of me.

At last the United trial date came. Mum and I took the train across the Pennines the day before and stayed in a small boarding house just South of Old Trafford. Uncle Alex stayed over too to make sure we found our way to the club on time the next morning. As if anybody wouldn't be able to find Old Trafford! But I suppose it's good to be careful. Uncle Alex mentioned being careful a few times. He was keen that we eat in the hotel and keep ourselves to ourselves. I suppose being associated with a big club he valued his privacy. So much for keeping a low profile though - he caused a right fuss as he almost choked on his dinner when I suggested that we could have stayed at his house with him and his wife.

The trial for United was different. We went to a special training ground and there must have been a hundred trialists from all over Britain and Ireland. My confidence disappeared in a minute. There were a couple of boys not much shorter than me. They all looked good and where some of them had footballs they were juggling them with their feet, knees and head. Two of them were heading the ball backwards and forwards to each other. I'd seen the professionals perform these sorts of tricks but these were lads of my own age.

A tall dark haired boy in a white shirt called out "to me!" as a ball fell at my feet and I swung a leg at it, trying to kick it back to the owner. But instead of caressing the ball into his hands it came off my ankle and flew straight into the back of the head of a bespectacled little fellow who was facing away from me. His thick rimmed glasses went flying off his head and landed in the grass a few feet away from him. As White-shirt trotted over to retrieve his ball he looked at me and loudly named me "wanker." I took little notice but, in an uncharacteristic moment of consideration, probably brought about by the realisation that I was completely out of my depth I went over to help the victim of my poor touch. He was on his hand and knees feeling for his glasses. Once he had put them on he looked around to see who was responsible and I just pointed to White-shirt as he dribbled away.

As this little fellow thanked me for my help I began to notice several things about him. The most obvious was that his eyesight must have been abysmal. He couldn't see his glasses when they were six feet away from him. Secondly although he was only about 5 foot 9 he was built like a brick out-house and thirdly he had a red track-suit on with a Manchester United badge above his heart. Nowadays of course everybody has club kit but in those days if you had the badge on then you were part of the club.

"Hello, I'm Harry. Are you trailing here?" I asked trying to open a conversation.

"No" he replied, still staring through his bottle-bottom glasses at White-shirt "I'm already an apprentice here. The way it works is that the best players are picked from the trialists and at the end of the day they play against a team from the club. So I'm here for that game."

"Um!" I said. I couldn't think of anything else to say. Take away his glasses and this fellow was the toughest looking player I'd ever seen up close. Having both of his front teeth missing added to the overall impression of grit. I was not sure if I wanted to be on the same pitch as him let alone the opposite side but at the same time if I didn't get through to the final game I'd be out. Things were not looking good. A whistle blew and we were called together by the coaches. So it was a quick "See you later, maybe" and off I went.

Things were very well organised. We spent the first thirty minutes "warming up" and stretching, holding each stretch for twenty seconds. We jogged and sprinted for about ten minutes and then we were split into groups of ten. Each group with a club coach. From the sacks that were strategically placed around the field about fifty footballs appeared and we were taken through a series of exercises. I was not doing particularly well. We were put into pairs and were knocking the ball to each other over a distance of ten metres when, for the third time, the ball span away from me and clashed with the ball of the next two players. They whined a complaint and the coach bellowed "For Christ Sake! Give the other boys a chance will you, son?" He made a note on his clipboard. I knew I'd had it.

But then my saviour arrived, and not too late, Uncle Alex, sporting a smart track-suit, walked over towards the coach and, as I continued the exercise, whispered in his ear. At first the coach was having none of it but then good old Uncle Alex whispered very closely in his ear and slipped something under the top sheet on the clipboard. The coach took a quick look at the delivery and with a furtive look around him nodded his assent. His next words were directed to me "That's right, lad, very good. There's no need to be nervous." And there wasn't. Not anymore and not yet, anyway.

The first period of the trials finished before lunch. We'd had lots of skill based exercises followed by a five-a-side game using small goals and half of a pitch. This is usually a game for the more skilful players rather than those of us who rely on a physical presence but I'd done OK by staying back and performing some last-ditch heroics. Our coach kept praising me and I noticed some of the other players were becoming unhappy. "What are you? His son?" asked one after I had been congratulated on a simple clearance. Sandwiches and a drink were provided but then came the selection for the next phase – a match between two selected teams. From each of the groups two or three players were selected. Those not selected were invited to stay, but for them the trial was over. Of course my name was the first one from our group, much to the chagrin of the other players in our set. They were obviously better judges of ability than the coach.

I was placed at centre-back for our team and I noticed the opposite centre-back was none other than White-shirt himself. The game kicked off and as my team was the stronger side I had plenty of opportunity to watch White-shirt in action. With only one centre-back and two full-backs it looked as if my main rival for a place in the next game was White-shirt and, damn, he was good! He had a way of winning the ball with ease; he'd curl his foot around it and drag it away from the opposition. He was fast, but worse than that instead of blindly humping the ball up the pitch à la Harry Barker he would look up and stroke the ball into the path of one of his own players. Fortunately his mid-field were outclassed and before you know it the ball was back in his penalty area and he was doing it all again. The game was intended to be a short twenty minutes each-way event but despite the pressure our team couldn't score. Suddenly the whole scenario changed. White-shirt had hit a long ball right over the top of our mid-field and a little ginger haired fellow had got on the end of it. He was running straight at me with the ball and there was nobody between him and our goalie but me. I had to stop him. He closed towards me and at the last moment feigned to drift right. My left leg stretched out to intercept the ball and with the simplest of ease he placed it between my legs. His accuracy was not complete because the ball deflected off my right leg away from his path. He had to slow down to collect the ball and that gave me my chance to turn and chase him. I was frantic. I'd had one thing to do in the whole game and this ginger-haired twit had made me look a fool. As we approached the penalty spot I caught a glimpse of the ball and imagined a fantastic tackle where I stole the ball from his foot just as he was taking his shot. That's what I imagined anyway. My leg went out. I felt contact. The whistle blew and from the ground I looked up to see the referee pointing at the spot while Ginger lay sprawled out on the ground.

And there he was, trotting up from the centre-back position to take the penalty - White-shirt. I hated this fellow but the thing was - I'd have done exactly the same myself.

We lost the game of course and when the eleven names were announced for the final match mine was not among them. I could see White-shirt jumping for joy. Isn't it wonderful that the best man won? Of course, but the game isn't over till the final whistle. Mum wasn't about so I thought I may as well hang around and watch the final game. I caught Uncle Alex's eye but he just shrugged his shoulders. Thinking back to the conversation that I had overheard in our parlour I walked over to him and whispered with a meaningful look "Mum will not be pleased." He shrugged his shoulders, turned his back, and walked to the touchline to watch the game that was just starting. I followed him. He was not getting away that easily.

White-shirt was at centre-back and as the game started the Trialists team were immediately put under pressure by the Apprentices. I could see my apprentice friend from earlier playing at Number 4. He was grafting in mid-field, winning the ball every time and passing comfortably to his team mates. When he needed to he used his strength. The Apprentices scored within a couple of minutes and then again on five minutes. White-shirt was playing well. He was putting in good tackles but that was not enough and then it happened. White-shirt had managed to intercept a through ball when the red Number 4 came through. It wasn't a dirty tackle but it was hard, very hard. Now White-shirt was no weakling but this Number 4 would be a World Class stopper in less than ten years. Having gone up in the air White-shirt eventually came down to land awkwardly on his shoulder with his arm twisted underneath his body. It was clear that he could not continue. Uncle Alex saw the opportunity even before I did. He grabbed my arm and we sprinted over to where the senior coaches were watching the game.

"Here is the other centre-back." he announced "If that lad can't continue why not put this lad on. They can't play a trial with only 10 players. That wouldn't be fair!"

(Oh! How I love that word "fair". It can be so useful)

The senior coaches looked at each other and the decision was made. I trotted on to take my place with probably the broadest smile I'd ever had. Good fortune? Maybe, but the first person to shake my hand was the Red Number 4. "It's one thing knocking my glasses off" he said, "but he shouldn't have called me names". Norbert Peter Styles was right – calling him anything other than Nobby or Mr Styles was a big mistake.

The injury to White-shirt and the two goal deficit had taken the wind out of the sails of most of the trialists but I had just been given a life-line and I was going to make the most of it. The Apprentices took it easy on us, they only scored a couple more, and I was able to put in some good challenges. My clearances were effective – although the ball did keep coming back into our area. I think my new friend Norbert had a word with his colleagues because they seemed to be giving me the space to play the ball rather than pressuring as they were the other players. They made me look good and I felt positive at the end of the game. The coaches sent us on our way with a promise that we'd hear in a week or so. Uncle Alex gave me the thumbs up and off I went, back to Leeds.

Moving On

Within a week I had received offers of an apprenticeship from all of the other clubs, except Bradford Park Avenue. Some phoned and some wrote letters. I am sure that the other clubs didn't know what they were looking for and that it was the simple fact that Manchester United wanted me that made them try to sign me up. The people at Park Avenue had got it right and looking back I would probably have fitted in there better than at any of the other clubs. Never mind. Their loss was my gain.

The only offer I was interested in was the one from Manchester United – to join them as an apprentice until the end of the season at which time my position would be reviewed. I would live in digs in Manchester and receive 10 shillings a week. I was not only nearly a professional footballer I was rich! My joy was only limited by news from Rose. Whilst I had been busy travelling and trailing she and Stan had resumed their relationship. It seems they were truly devoted to each other after all. I couldn't stand in the way of "True Love" now could I? And, anyway, once I got to Manchester there'd be girls galore. Stan was now back in training and hoping to become a professional footballer. I gave him the phone number of Bradford Park Avenue.

After I arrived in Manchester I was afraid that my lack of talent would be found out very quickly, but it wasn't. I could keep up with the training runs and if I concentrated I didn't make too much of a fool of myself in the practice matches.

A few weeks after my arrival, Manchester United was struck by the worst tragedy the club has experienced. The Munich Air Disaster on February 6th 1958.

I am not the person and this is not the place to talk about that.

The PFA

For the next few years I managed to stay in the background. The club needed to re-build so the main focus was on bringing experienced players into the first team. Now when I started as a Pro I thought ten bob a week would be plenty but I soon found that with the price of beer and gin ten bob didn't go very far, even in 1960. The problem was that unless I could make my way into, well, at least the reserves, I wouldn't earn a penny more. Every week I was paying the compulsory three-pence to the Professional Footballers Association so when I heard that their chairman was coming up from London to Manchester to talk to the players I thought it'd be a good idea to have a chat. I mean there were girls out there who got quite friendly after three gins – and sometimes I could only afford two! I'd like to find out what was happening to my three-pence (I could get a pint or the third gin for that) and maybe negotiate a discount.

So after training one Tuesday those that were interested, which was about half a dozen of us, made our way to the Church Hall at St Bride's and sat amongst twenty to thirty or so players from other local clubs like City, Stockport County, Bury and Bolton. The older players all knew each other of course and there was no sign of the rivalry and aggression that appeared on the pitch. We all sat around chatting and the older players introduced the younger ones to their friends from other clubs. There were two players from the lower league clubs who were clearly, shall we say, less well-dressed than the players from the bigger clubs. Their shoes well-worn and their jackets and ties had clearly seen better days. These men were family men in their mid-thirties. Their careers were coming to an end as their best playing and earning days were well behind them. If these players couldn't find a job in football their next step would be back into the factories, if they were lucky. If things didn't change that could be me in fifteen years time! I took note.

An immaculately dressed fellow, tall and slim, arrived and pressed the flesh around the room. My attention was firstly caught by the quality of his clothes – whatever this fellow did for a living it paid well and then I noticed a quite remarkable facial feature – he had the biggest chin that I had ever seen in my life. He seemed to know all of the senior players and eventually made his way to the small stage area at the head of the room. Having welcomed the new members, and introduced himself as Jimmy, he proceeded to give a speech about the history of the PFA and how it had its roots in Manchester and how it had been protecting player rights for donkey's years and something about a strike in 1909 and on and on. I listened intently for as long as I could but as he began his second sentence my attention was once again drawn to his enormous chin. As he spoke he also moved his head to make eye contact with individual members of the audience so his chin moved from side-to-side and up and down like a conductor's baton. I was transfixed by this movement and gradually my eyes began to close. I had been out quite late the previous night with a rather large lass called Doreen. She was not the best looking girl in Manchester but she drank "mild" and lacked the capacity for more than a couple. I had fallen on very hard times you see. Doreen was not my kind of girl but sitting with her was better than sitting alone in my bed-sit. Just.

Jimmy droned on for what seemed like a lifetime but was probably only four or five years and then there was silence. At that moment my eyes closed and I felt myself falling from my chair. Sub-consciously my muscles reacted and forced me awake and with a strangled snore as I sat upright in the chair only to see Jimmy looking straight at me from the stage.

"Yes?" he asked "You have a question?"

Everybody in the room was looking at me expectantly. It seemed a few of them had been woken by the change of tempo too. I think they were hoping for a more interesting topic of conversation than whatever this fellow was going on about. He seemed a pleasant enough bloke, I thought, but I didn't like the way his chin was pointing accusingly at me.

"Were you going to add something?" Jimmy wondered "I'd be interested in hearing the ideas of the younger generation of footballers".

I still looked at him blankly. Whilst the situation was not unfamiliar to me – I had fallen asleep many times in class at school but his reaction was different to that of the teachers whose usual ploy to wake sleeping pupils was to lob a blackboard eraser at the miscreant and then give them a thrashing. (Their poor aim was an effective deterrent because when the wooden eraser was thrown anybody could be hit, so pupils around the sleeper would be keen to wake them up. A fine example of effective post-war educational psychology, but I digress.)

He gave me a clue. "Do you question whether we should challenge the legitimacy of the Retain and Transfer system so that our members will be free to move to other clubs like any other free citizen of England or should we allow our owners the right to buy and sell us like slaves?"

Now I know a loaded question when I hear one and if you are interested in the history of football to see how it has moved from one extreme - where once you had signed for a club you were theirs to do with as they please (and clubs would sell players to other clubs hundreds of miles away without the player's agreement) to the other extreme following the Bosman ruling where players can move where they like and the clubs can't build strategically over a period of years because they don't know if their key players will chose to leave at any minute. And now even I am beginning to sound like Jimmy.

At this point one of the less well-dressed players found the will to join the debate. He clearly didn't agree with Jimmy in fact he clearly thought it was bollocks.

"That's Bollocks!" he cried and sat down convinced that he'd made his point and awaited the riposte to his argument from Jimmy.

Jimmy struggled to form a reply and as he paused another fellow from the lower leagues stood up "It's all very well for you lot from down South or from the big clubs up here but what about us? The clubs own our registration so they look after us. If we get injured we still get half pay and when players lose their form they get transferred down the leagues. We still get paid in the summer and can get work locally. I've only got four or five years left of my career" (I think he was exaggerating there from the way he was walking I reckon if he'd been a horse they'd have shot him) "and who's going to find me a job at the end of my career if the clubs don't?"

These were pretty good arguments and the crowd were very much awake now and looked to Jimmy for his answer. Jimmy hadn't expected this kind of response to what he considered to be a won debate, so he was taken aback. Then, seeing his escape route, he deflected the group's attention onto me.

"Hold on, hold on! Let's hear what the young fellow has to say".

I'd had time now to gather my thoughts and decided now was the time to bring up the question of my three-pence. Public speaking wasn't my forte but I decided to give it a go.

"It's about the money, you see…." But I got no further because all around me there was uproar.

"The young fella's right"

"He's hit the hammer on the head"

"Exactly. That's what it's all about"

"Good 'un, the young lad."

Apparently they all had a problem with the three-pence.

"Go on, young fella – tell him." They were all looking at me and I felt I had to stand up. So I did.

"You see. I'm an apprentice at Manchester United and I've been getting ten bob a week for the last two years." They were all listening intently and Jimmy was nodding his head. "I can't live on that, you see." There was agreement all around the room so I thought it was time to get to the point. "I pay three-pence a week into the PFA and I want to know what I'm getting for my money."

Once again I seemed to have hit the hammer on the head because there were "Hear! Hear!" and "Well said!" and "Yes, what do we get for our money?" coming from all over the room.

Jimmy was now under a bit of pressure. He knew things were going badly and if he didn't deal with this young firebrand then the whole PFA could be undermined. His job as chairman could be on the line. He needed to take control of this meeting before it got out of hand.

"Now hold on lads." he said "You know I'm one of you. The way the clubs work is all based on which team you play for. The top players can only earn the maximum wage - £20 per week - so the next best players earn a bit less, the reserves and lower league players a bit less all the way down to the apprentices who are lucky to get ten bob. That's just how it is."

From the back a voice called "Well what you going to do about this lad, then?"

"Well, I don't know." he answered and then looking at me "What do you want me to do?"

I'd followed the discussion so far and the problem seemed to me that because there was a £20 limit on what the top players earned then I could only earn ten bob. So the answer seemed simple.

"I want you to get rid of the maximum wage so we can all get a bit more." I replied and there was silence, for about half a second and then once again the room erupted. Cheers and "He's right again" and "Yes, that's what we want" and Jimmy calling for order.

"Order, Order!" he cried "Is that the feeling of the meeting?" he asked, going with the flow. There was a unanimous chorus of "Ayes".

"Alright then, your PFA is behind you in getting the maximum wage abolished." the room sensed a twist "But how are we going to make the clubs agree? A strike?"

Now Jimmy had played his ace. Nobody in the room wanted a strike, especially the low paid. Jimmy scanned the room, challenging for an answer to his question.

"I can't afford to go on strike." Confirmed the Bollocks Man.

"The clubs would use that as an excuse to sack some of us." an older player observed.

"They'd keep the better players on though wouldn't they? The Internationals and so on and just sack the other players."

"They might even decide to pay us less money."

Jimmy had taken control of the room and felt it was now time to silence the main dissenter he looked at his rival and in an attempt to fully establish his command he asked "Well, young fellow, do you want everybody to go on strike and lose their livelihoods that keep their families fed?"

I knew that the right answer wasn't that I didn't care about these other players and their families I just wanted to afford the price of a third gin now and again so I searched for a solution. I looked for a hole in his claim "They wouldn't ALL lose their jobs." I replied. "As that fellow said – they wouldn't sack the Internationals."

It seems that this time I had not only struck the metal pin firmly with the hard-headed tool designed specifically for the purpose but driven it finally into place. Once again the room acknowledged my brilliance. "Of course! Only the England Internationals would strike if the maximum wage was not abolished." "They would agree to it because they had the most to gain". "The boy is a genius". I was briefly concerned that they would lift me onto their shoulders and march down to London to lay siege to Parliament when Jimmy finally called them to order. He knew when he was beaten.

"The proposal is" he announced "that the PFA demand that the Maximum Wage of £20 is abolished. All those in favour?" It was unanimous.

"Very well" said Jimmy "I shall take that to the PFA committee. Now about the Retain and Transfer system" but by then by popular opinion the meeting was over and I was invited to join my colleagues in the local pub where we remained until closing time.

Jimmy Hill made his way back to London with his instructions from the North and I woke the next morning with a hangover but still no wiser about what I was getting for my three-pence.

The Best and the Worst of Us

Jimmy went on to have a pretty successful career. He did some television, managed some clubs and became the Chairman of Coventry City. Although I think the highlight was when he took over the linesman's flag at The Arsenal – and it was all built on his fame as the man who fought and won the abolition of the maximum wage for players. So we now have players who earn more in a week than some people earn in ten years. I mean, it's not as if they are boys from public schools managing funds in the City of London they're just working class lads who've got lucky. I am happy for him to take the credit for that.

Meanwhile I gained quite a reputation from my first meeting of the PFA and players would often come to me for advice on all sorts of matters. I suppose I was "building a reputation". It wasn't difficult to tell people what they wanted to hear. People usually know what they want to do; they just need someone to tell them they should do it.

When, in 1961, another group of trialists were brought together at the club I took my place among the apprentices ready to show them how it should be done. Our places could be under threat if the trialists outshone us but I wasn't too worried. The quality of our forwards and midfield meant that few, if any of the opposition would get through and if they did I'd be there to stop them getting any further. I'd only have to catch them once!

I turned up a little late at the training ground sporting a mild hangover from the night before but nothing that would stop me putting my head on a ball, or an opposition player. As I entered the changing room I adopted my usual confident stride – you have to look the part and let them know the guv'nor has arrived.

"Alright Lads" I announced but instead of receiving my usual greeting of "Alright Harry" there was a huge roar of laughter. My immediate thought was that they'd lost their senses and somebody was going to need a good hiding but surely they hadn't forgotten the lessons I'd been teaching them over the last two years? On the pitch and in the changing room I am the Guv'nor – and some of them had the bruises and scars to remind them. But I soon realised there was still some sense left in the world. It wasn't me that was the object of their ridicule. Behind the door a small dark haired figure was crouching in an attempt to hide the fact that he was naked from the waist down. Across the room one of the bigger apprentices was waving a pair of white shorts around his head. The little fellow looked up at me and with a broad Irish accent said "Thank Jasus. I t'ought yo' was the boss".

I am, I thought, and before anybody gets any ideas to the contrary I'd better impose myself on this situation. "Ok" I said ensuring I had everybody's attention. "Let the little fella have his kaks back." Of course there was no argument and the white shorts were thrown unceremoniously across the room to the little Irishman. He whipped them on quickly and stood up to face my chest.

"T'anks a lot. Oim Georgie" he said quietly offering his hand. "You're welcome" I replied realising that I was shaking the hand that had just been used to cover his groin. "I'm Harry Barker. Now you sit over there" I said pointing to a small gap near where I would change "and I'll keep an eye on you."

For some reason I'd taken a liking to Georgie. He had a certain glint in his eye and a quiet manner, quite the opposite to me, and I just thought there'd be no harm in looking after him. Harry the Magnanimous – that's me!

The rowdy behaviour resumed amongst the apprentices while Georgie and the other trialists prepared themselves and sat nervously waiting for the coach to call us out onto the pitch. It was a bright, warm afternoon, and the sun was low in the sky. The teams lined up and I noticed little Georgie was playing up front. Well, I may have helped him in the changing room but if he came near me on the pitch he'd get the same as everybody else I decided. Of course the apprentices put the trialists under pressure from the off and within a couple of minutes we were one up. I settled into my role of patrolling our half of the pitch and felt comfortable as the rest of my team went forward. Enjoy yourself I thought and keep them all up the other end. But what's this? Somebody has hoofed the ball towards our half and it looks as if little Georgie is racing with one of our midfielders for the ball. Not a problem, thinks I, that's our ball but then as quick as a whippet Georgie has stolen the ball off the foot of our player and is running forward with it. Sorry Georgie, you're getting no further forward than me, and I placed myself between him and our goal as I had done so many times to so many forwards. I'd better not hurt him though, just enough to slow him down for the rest of the game.

Georgie approached me. Didn't he have more sense? I kept my eye on the ball and he kept the ball close to his feet. Then I saw my chance, he'd put the ball just a few inches too far ahead of himself. It'll be a lunge with my right foot to stop him and then bring my left leg over the back of his calves to scissor him to the ground. No problem. Sorry Georgie..

So out went my right leg and the left followed through and made contact with …. nothing! I couldn't believe it. He was there… had he vanished into thin air? I looked around in time to see that Georgie had re-materialised in our penalty area and was in the process of taking the ball around our goalkeeper and tapping it into the net. Like a seasoned pro I immediately shifted the blame onto the midfield.

"Where were you? I asked. "I can't do it all by myself! You've got to give me some cover!"

The goalkeeper took my cue and added a twist. "Where was the defence?" he asked. "You've left me wide open." Then the midfield joined in. "Come on you forwards. We've got to defend from the front."

Oh Yes! We were all schooled in the art of survival in sport.

Back to kick-off and the apprentices were suddenly a lot less confident. Two of them went for the same ball and it fell loose. Georgie picked it up and was off at a gallop. One of the midfielders, determined not to be too slow off the mark and having seen that Georgie was likely to get through again, immediately started to apportion blame.

"Come on Harry. You've got to close him down!"

I admired his escalation of the blame-tactic from blaming after the event to blaming others before things had even gone wrong. I decided to learn from that but first I had to stop Georgie. There was only one thing for it. As I ran I suddenly pulled up sharp and dropped to the ground. Georgie went through and curled the ball past our keeper while I lay on the ground rubbing my left calf. A trainer jogged on.

"What's wrong?" he asked.

"Something seemed to pull as I was about to accelerate. I don't think I can carry on."

"Let me take a look!" and he lifted my right foot into the air.

"Ouch! Ouch!" I cried. "Take it easy!"

"Hang on a moment." The trainer looked at me with a knowing look. "It was your left leg that you were rubbing just now."

Damn. Fancy me falling for that. "They both hurt" I lied.

"Right" he said "well how about you get up and run about a bit to see if it improves. Maybe you could start by trying to catch up with that little Irish lad."

The old fool had me sussed.

"No problem, chum. I would have caught him that time if my leg hadn't gone."

"Right then. Off you go and let me see you do it." And with that he splashed a freezing cold, wet sponge on my privates. I, of course, jumped up from the ground as the shock of the cold water hit me. Oh Yes! The Magic Sponge works every time!

As the trainer left the field Georgie, who had been hanging around so see how I was, came over and asked if I was alright.

"Yep I'm fine Georgie" I said seeing my chance "but I'm a bit worried about you."

"Why?" he asked.

"Look, Georgie. See these players around us? Well if you pass the trials – and after two goals you're as good as through – all these guys are going to be your team-mates. And here you are making them all look really bad. You've got to take it easy. You've done enough already. Remember these are going to be your mates and you know how things were in the changing rooms before I came in?" I shook my head solemnly thinking now was a good time to remind him that he owed me a favour.

"I'll tell you what. Next time you're through let me win the ball and maybe let me catch you a couple of times. You've got to learn to get along with people, Georgie."

He nodded and trotted off. Nobody else had heard our conversation so the apprentices in mid-field kept tight on Georgie, as best they could, but the inevitable soon happened and Georgie was away. As he bore down on me I wondered if he would have taken my good advice to heart. We'd soon see.

Georgie was fast. He'd left the mid-field behind and they had lined me up as a scapegoat already.

"Your ball, Harry" from central mid-field and "Pass it wide when you get it Harry" from the left wing. Sarcastic git, I thought.

He was close now and I focussed on the ball. I can do this, I thought and the ball moved from his left foot to his right and I saw a chance. I lunged. I was going to get it.... and then his left foot appeared as a flash and he touched the ball three inches to my right. I knew I'd missed. He'd done me like a kipper. I fell to the ground; my right leg outstretched and felt something roll up to my, still soaking, groin. I looked down to see the ball resting between my legs and Georgie, well he was gone. Up I jumped and played the ball out to the left wing. It's an art you know, to play a ball just a little too far so the other player looks bad when he doesn't get it. A little bit of top-spin helps. I'd nearly perfected that skill and sure enough our left winger chased the ball but failed to keep it in. He knew what I'd done, but his sarcasm had to be punished. Look after your team-mates, sure, but look after yourself first.

"Try to keep up with the game you lazy bastard!" I called out to the wing. He flicked a two-fingered response.

I felt a light tap on my shoulder as Georgie trotted by. "Well done" he said, and gave me a wink. I'm going to like this guy, I thought, and the way things are working out it looks like we're going to need somebody to play out on the left.

Of course Georgie breezed through the trial. He didn't score another goal and a couple of times allowed me to catch him on his runs. I came off the field feeling pretty good and, of course, gave the trainer, who was shaking his head in disbelief, a broad smile as I walked past.

Georgie moved into digs in the next street so it seemed quite natural that we'd walk home together after training. I was fully occupied most evenings with various dates and was particularly keen on a girl who had recently moved to Manchester from Wales. This girl, Jackie, had befriended Doreen so I was hoping that an introduction could be made. I'd had some difficulty because Doreen seemed to be a bit keen on me herself and didn't seem to be equally keen to introduce me to her slim, beautiful, dark-haired friend. I can't think why.

What I needed was a diversion and a plan formed wherein quiet, shy Georgie would provide the answer. Doreen worked on the sweet counter in Woolworth's on King's Road. Not a good choice of occupation for somebody with her tendency towards over-eating. I met her there one evening when she had finished work and suggested that I walk her home. She was ecstatic at the idea and perhaps I should have taken that as a warning but I was so engrossed in my plan that I didn't heed the signs. I took her persistent attempts to hold my hand and continually bumping into me to be a result of her losing her balance and wanting help to keep upright and on course.

On the way back, through the narrow terraced side-streets, I explained to Doreen how little Georgie has come all the way from his home in Ireland and was feeling very lonesome. He spent too much time alone in the evenings in his digs. He should get out more and what he needed was a girl-friend. So how about we make up a four-some? Georgie, me, you and maybe, that Jackie. I'm sure <u>you</u> get the picture but just to spell it out: Doreen, you see, was a generous girl and very likely to introduce Georgie to a woman's ways. That'd do him good and leave me with a clear run on Jackie. After Doreen agreed I rubbed my hands together with glee.

When we arrived at her house all the lights were off. "Oh! I see nobody's at home. Would you like to come in for a bit?" she asked.

"A bit of what?" I laughed.

"You know!" she winked and, bloody hell, I think she was serious! God help little Georgie, I thought.

Fortunately at this point the door opened and I saw the shadow of a large, burly man about the width of my father but taller by six inches.

"Is that you, Doreen?" he growled. "Have you got somebody there with you?"

"No Dad" she lied "It's just 'arry"

"I ain't 'aving you bring any lads home. If I catch any of them layabouts 'anging around 'ere I'll punch the living daylights out of them and don't you 'ave any of 'em 'ere while I'm away, either. Now, 'ave you got a tanner for the meter?"

Doreen reached into her purse and found six-pence for her father. We agreed to meet on Saturday at seven outside Woolworths. I heard her father bellowing something about Saturday as he fed the electricity meter and every light in the house came on. A huge shadow eclipsed the front doorway. I made sure that I was long gone before he closed the front door. So far, so good. Next was Georgie.

Persuading Georgie to come out on the Saturday night was not as easy as I thought it would be.

"But I promised I'd write a letter to me Mam on a Saturday, I promised!" I had never heard such a feeble excuse.

"What is it? The pens don't work on a Sunday?" I enquired. "Come on Georgie, there's more to life than football"

"Like what?"

That was an easy one "Like having a bet, or maybe having a drink, or dancing and girls. There are loads of things to do – you like good clothes don't you Georgie? You've got to live a little. Football's just what we do to get us the things that we want, Georgie." I put my arm around him and gave him a friendly hug. I needed him outside Woolworths on Saturday at Seven O'clock. If he didn't get on with Doreen and never wanted to see her or go out ever again I didn't care; but on Saturday at Seven O'clock I <u>needed</u> Georgie outside Woolworths.

"I like football. Playing football is all I've ever want to do."

I knew then that I had him. "But Georgie" I reasoned "have you ever tried these things. Have you been out and had a good time with the girls, Georgie?"

He shook his head.

"So why not come out with me on Saturday? If it doesn't work out you can be back in your digs by eight o'clock and you can write to your Mam and tell her all about it. Come on, Georgie. Give it a try."

I gave him my best, encouraging smile and he smiled back and gave me a nod. Saturday night was on and I reckoned that Doreen was going to make sure little Georgie enjoyed himself in a way that I couldn't see making its way into a letter to Mrs Best!

We played a match on Saturday afternoon and Georgie was a star. He got a goal and ran their back line ragged. The manager was there to watch him and the coach was very pleased. Everybody was smiling but none more than me. We had a shower and I arranged to collect

Georgie from his digs at half past six. It was only a fifteen minute walk to Woolworth's but I wanted to leave plenty of time in case Georgie needed some more persuasion. I didn't expect to find what I did when I arrived at the digs. George was ready to go ... to Church. He looked like a little lost lamb in his pale-blue button-up cardigan over his white shirt which was primly buttoned up under his chin. I double-checked to make sure he wasn't wearing short-trousers.

"What on earth are you wearing, Georgie?" It was too late to do anything about it now. I could have lent Georgie some things but he would have looked ridiculous in my over-large clothes. The first thing you've got to do next week, Georgie, is to get yourself some decent clothes. I don't ever want to see you dressed like that again! You're letting yourself down." He looked upset so I thought I'd better boost his confidence some. I needed him, you see. "You're going to be a big success around here and people are going to expect you to look like one. You've got to set the trends, Georgie."

"Thanks, Harry. You're a pal" he smiled and I placed my hand on his shoulder.

"Now come on. We've got some girls to meet!"

Doreen and Jackie arrived just a few minutes late. Not bad for girls, I thought. They must be keen. "Shall we get a drink before we go to the pictures?" I suggested. There were no arguments and off we went to the pub. Doreen had half a pint of mild and Jackie had a gin and lime. I took a pint of Best and Georgie wanted a lemonade. I gave him the "Come on Georgie for God's sake" look and he changed it to half of best. I got him a pint. Things were going quite well and we decided to stay in the pub rather than go to the cinema. Everybody was very friendly but I couldn't seem to engage Jackie in conversation. Doreen kept interrupting and even when I asked Jackie about Wales Doreen was the one that told me all about it. Georgie, meanwhile, sat quietly, occasionally sipping his drink and looking shyly at Jackie. A few rounds later I'd started to feel the drink. Doreen had gone onto the gin and

Jackie found she had to lean close to Georgie to hear what the quiet man had to say.

We needed to move on, I thought. Maybe we should go to a club or the late show at the cinema after the next round. Doreen took another gin and I had a pint. Georgie and Jackie had hardly touched their last drinks so Doreen and I finished them. Then it was time to go and the four of us made our way to the door. I followed Doreen and Jackie out into the cold night air. Suddenly Doreen fell backwards into my arms. Her eyes were glazed and her muscles relaxed. She was completely plastered and looking up at me she slurred "'ello. What you doing up there?" and burst into a fit of giggles and belched alcohol fumes into my face. "Sorry." She croaked and giggled again. I think she was trying to be cute and seductive.

This was not what I had planned. I'd had a bit to drink but this was ridiculous. No wonder she usually only drank a couple of halves of mild, but things could still work out.

I pulled Georgie aside and rested Doreen on a ledge in the doorway. "Georgie. You'll have to take Doreen home."

Georgie as amiable as ever said "Sure, no problem." Good lad!

I followed through "We can't leave Jackie out here on her own so late at night so I'll walk her home. Ok?"

"Foine" says Georgie. It was settled.

"Jackie." I explained "Georgie is going to take Doreen home so I'd better walk you back to your place."

Jackie didn't look keen but clearly there was no other choice. I added "It wouldn't be gentlemanly to leave you out here alone now, would it?"

To press the point home I poured the unresisting but highly resistable Doreen into Georgie's arms only to see him collapse under her weight.

"It's no good" he groaned "I can't hold her."

"You'll have to take her" Jackie suggested giving me a fiery, defiant Celtic stare with her deep, dark brown eyes making my blood run hot with desire. (Mills & Boon take note.)

I could see it wasn't going to work out with Georgie taking Doreen so I conceded the point. "Alright. I'll take Doreen home and meet you back here in about half an hour." I could then dismiss Georgie from his duties leaving Jackie and I to enjoy the rest of the evening. All was not yet lost.

They agreed so I set off along King's Road with Doreen in tow. It took much longer than I expected to get back to her house. Not the least because every few yards she insisted on stopping to tell me how much she "really, really, really loved me" and that I was "the only fella she had ever really, really, really loved." Yes, I thought, well thank you for that but while we are meandering through the streets of Manchester there's an incredibly beautiful young woman waiting for me so if you could waddle a little quicker it'd be much appreciated.

Eventually we reached her house and I banged on the door while she searched for her key. "It's no good" she said "Dad's on nights." She eventually found her key but was unable to find the lock. I was losing patience by now so I roughly took the key out of her hand and opened the door. "Fank you" she breathed "you'd better come in" and with that she shoved me through the door.

"Hold on." I said "I've got to go."

She didn't answer but flicked at the light switch. Nothing happened. "Bugger" she said "'ave you got a sixpence?"

I didn't. So I said so.

"There's one upstairs. I'll get it." she said and promptly fell to her knees.

Now it wasn't that I'd forgotten about Jackie or that I had an overwhelming desire to behave gentlemanly, it was the fact that she had collapsed in the doorway and the only thing I could think to do would be to get the lights on and to get out of there.

"Ok" I said "I'll get it." and I set off up the stairs but when I reached the top I realised that I had no chance of finding a sixpence in a strange house in the dark. So I ran back down again. "Where is it?" I asked.

"I'll show you" she said and lifted her head off the floor only for it to slump back down again. So I raised her as best I could and carried her in a fireman's lift up the stairs. She pointed feebly to a room and I carried her in, my knees buckling under the weight. In the half-light of a nearby street lamp she indicated a bed-side table. I looked around to see where to drop her so I could find the coin. The floor looked tempting but the bed was just as close so I sat her on the edge of the bed and allowed her to fall back onto the covers. I could then use my hands to feel across the top of the bed-side table for the money.

Suddenly a woman's voice called from downstairs. "Hello. Is there anybody there? The door was open." The voice had startled me and my hand knocked against a glass that some fool had left on the table. It fell to the floor and smashed. "Who is that? Is that burglars?" A moment's silence. Then the woman's shrill voice screamed "Help! Help! Call the police! Burglars!" And then a second voice, a man and another woman "What is it?" "It's a burglar. The door was open and I heard something smash upstairs."

"I'll go up" said the man.

"No, No." Another woman's voice. "He might be violent"

"I'll take this" says he. Now I didn't know what "this" was but I didn't fancy being on the wrong end of it. I looked around. Doreen snored. I should walk down and explain everything. Doreen was drunk and I was upstairs in her room... doing what exactly? Not a good option, I thought. The hero downstairs might decide to use "this" and then talk about it later.

The window. It opened quite easily.

"Alright. Alright. Everybody back now." An authoritative voice took command. "What's all this going on 'ere then?"

Great. I thought. Now we'd got Dixon of Dock Green downstairs.

I looked out of the window while a gabble of voices put the policeman in the picture.

Then, one high-pitched woman's voice, louder than the rest. "What if he's got that poor innocent little girl up there?"

There were gasps from below as the local population considered the unthinkable – and trust me – if you'd seen her sprawled on the bed like a rejected walrus you'd know just how unthinkable it was. Quite naturally and taking her cue to confirm matters the "poor innocent little girl" farted.

There was a clamour downstairs led by a man's voice. They'd delayed long enough and Dixon of Dock Green was leading a charge up the stairs to rescue the damsel in distress. "Follow Me!" he cried imagining, no doubt, himself to be leading a group of heroic warriors attacking an well entrenched, powerful enemy against incredible odds the like of which the Charge of the Light Brigade would be considered an annoyingly interrupted country-side frolic.

There was no option. Faced with the choice of at least a night in the cells — that wouldn't have got me back to Jackie in time — or a leap into the unknown I took a more cautious route and clambered out of the window and lowered myself onto the roof of the outside toilet. I am not sure if the prison could have held me but soon found out that the roof of the toilet couldn't. I crashed through the corrugated asbestos roof. (Dangerous stuff, asbestos. Why put it on the roof of a toilet? Fireproof bogs? I am not sure that bears thinking about.) I landed one foot in the pan while the other twisted on the concrete floor. I could hear my pursuers in the room above.

The same penetrating woman's voice "He's murdered the poor girl!" More screams and Dixon of Dock Green blew his whistle three times. That shut them up but it was also the signal for any copper in the area to come running to his assistance.

I got out of the toilet as quickly as I was able. I could hear hands trying to open the back door of the house from the inside but it was securely locked. (That shows you what kind of area this was.) I hobbled the short length of the back yard and opened a gate onto a narrow alley-way. I'd hurt my ankle but the fear inside me was too great for me to let that slow me down — much. I ran. But not too far, you see running attracts people's attention so, having turned right into the alley, as soon as I got a hundred yards from the house I turned left at the first street and left again then walked parallel to the street with all the commotion, effectively closer to the house that I had just left. A policeman ran past, breathing heavily. I paused and watched him run past me, just as any innocent bystander would. This route took me further away from the pub in King's Road but eventually I'd make my way back there. My ankle was painful, but it would be worth it. That Jackie was a very beautiful girl.

I was not paying sufficient attention to the road and was nearly killed for my lack of awareness. Just as I stepped out to cross the side-street some drunk lunatic, clearly going too fast, nearly run me down. Fortunately he managed to brake and swerve and I think hit something solid. I didn't hang around to find out what.

I had to take a wide circular route so the pub had closed long before I returned and much to my surprise Georgie and Jackie were nowhere to be found. I know it was almost two hours ago but I distinctly remember that we'd agreed they would wait for me. I searched for a while and then returned to my digs. My ankle had swollen and was becoming more painful. I was glad to get into bed that night. I decided to have a word with Georgie in the morning. If he is going to get on in this world he's going to have to learn to be more reliable. I decided to have a very serious talk with him about that but, sadly, events overtook us and we never did have that conversation.

When Georgie came round to my digs the following morning I couldn't be angry with him. He was bubbling. It was brilliant he said. He and Jackie had waited for ages for me to return and then she had insisted that he walk her home. They'd got some chips on the way and she'd invited him in for coffee.

Georgie explained with a twinkle that he'd never had coffee before.

I didn't want to hear any more.

Worse was to come for me. My ankle was bad so I went to see the club doctor on Monday morning, telling him I'd twisted it in the game on Saturday. He wrapped it in a tight dressing and told me to rest it. I should also try an alternating hot and cold water treatment to reduce the swelling. I suppose that was better than an ice-cold sponge to the groin.

I had to sit through watching the others train. Georgie was amazing. I had never watched him from the side-lines before. The coaches weren't impressed though. I heard them calling "What's wrong, Georgie? You're a bit off the pace today. Did you have a heavy weekend?" They laughed. I didn't. Georgie had seen Jackie on Sunday evening too and she had told him that once Doreen had sobered up her father had been told the whole story. I was worried. The club was a bit old fashioned in its attitude towards its junior staff picking up injuries when falling through the roofs of toilets having been chased out of the window of a drunken girl's bedroom. I suppose even these days that might raise an eyebrow or two.

The training session ended as the Austin A40 of the head-coach pulled up. "Georgie" he smiled "the Boss wants a word. I'll give you a lift." He then turned to me and added "He wants you too, Barker." I knew there was trouble. As we pulled out of the training ground we almost struck a large man in a donkey jacket who was striding aggressively through the gates. For a moment I thought I recognised him but had other things on my mind. I had never been called to the boss's office before and I did not think this was good news. Georgie sat in the back of the A40 grinning his simple smile. "Oh! What it must be to be innocent", I dreamed and gave Georgie a thumbs up and a smile. He responded similarly.

We were told to wait on the chairs outside Mr Busby's office. I was too nervous even to make a play for the attractive secretary who took the time between filing and deflecting phone calls to give Georgie a come-on smile. Georgie gave her his shy-boy look and I reckon if I hadn't been in the room she'd have been all over him in a moment. On the coffee table in front of me were several photos of first team players. I noticed the head-shot of Bobby Charlton. Even as a young man he had started to lose his hair and was quite bald on the top of his head. I looked at the photo and wondered what he would look like with a full head of hair. There was a pencil on the coffee table so I absent-mindedly picked it up and drew hair, coming from the side right over the top of his head. It took years off him. The door to the office opened and out came the man himself, Bobby Charlton. He was an established first team regular and England International so we had not come into contact with each other over the two years that I had been at the club, although I had seen him from a distance. I dropped the pencil and photograph. Bobby noticed them fall and reached to pick up the photo. I tried to get to it first but he was ahead of me. He looked at the photo, and looked at me, then at the photo again. He smiled. "Thanks" he said, and left clasping the vandalised snap.

Georgie was called in first. I tried to listen but the thick panelled door kept what was said in that room confidential. After about five minutes Georgie came out smiling the broadest grin I had ever seen. He walked over to me and grasped my arms – "I'm in!" he whispered "I'm in the first team squad!" If he was pleased then I was elated. So that is what this was about, at last I'm going to be getting some real money.

"You're next." the secretary directed me to the door and as I walked through I noticed she had walked over to congratulate Georgie and planted a kiss on his cheek. Take it easy Georgie. One at a time! You've got to keep your strength up.

Mr Busby was sitting behind a polished wooden desk. I stood almost to attention facing him. I remember the desk was well organised with a black telephone and a few papers positioned squarely but I got the impression that Mr Busby didn't feel comfortable there. The head coach was standing against the wall to his left. Mr Busby turned to him and said "I think he has probably finished his cup of tea now. Would you bring him up?" The head-coach nodded and left the room.

"Well" said Mr Busby "How do you think you are getting on here?"

"Pretty good" I answered "I reckon I could be ready for a chance with the first team."

"Do you?" He seemed a bit surprised and his eyebrows lifted. "Yes, I think you may be ready for first team football. You're nearly twenty now I think?"

That was right and I sensed this was it. At last I was going to be in the big money.

"But you've got an injury, I see. The ankle. How did that come about?"

He was well-informed, I thought, but then that's his job.

"Oh it's nothing. I just twisted it in a match on Saturday."

At that moment the door opened and in came the head coach followed by a very unwelcome sight. A police sergeant, note-book and all, stepped through the door. He had removed his helmet.

"Thank you very much, Mr Busby. Very nice cup of tea, thank you."

"You're welcome, Sergeant. Now would you like a seat?" But he preferred to stand. The court, it seemed, was in session.

Now I hope I haven't given you the impression that I was such a fool as to think that Manchester United always had a police sergeant present when handing out first team places. As soon as he entered the room I knew I was in trouble. I shan't repeat every word that was said although even now I can remember it vividly.

The police sergeant opened the batting "Mr Barker?"

I nodded.

"Saturday night there was a break-in at the home of a Mr Brennan in Royston Road. Some damage was caused and we have reports of an attempted assault on Mr Brennan's daughter. I wonder if you could help us with our enquiries?"

At times like this, I decided, you have to tell the truth, so I did "But what has this got to do with me?" I asked "I don't know this Mr Brennan" (which was true) "and I don't even fancy, Doreen" (which was also true) "so why would I be up in her bedroom?"

But it goes to show you that the truth doesn't always help. Mr Busby put his head in his hands while the head coach looked at the ceiling and sighed. The policeman continued.

"Fortunately for you, young man, Miss Brennan has explained how she was taken ill whilst out with friends and how you were kind enough to see her home. She insists that you acted as a perfect gentleman throughout." Hang on, I thought, I've got a reputation to uphold.

"There was" Plod continued, "some damage at the property. A glass water-jug" (so that's what it was) "and the roof of the outside toilet. Mr Brennan is insistent that the damage be paid for and" he turned to me "you should know, my lad, Mr Brennan is, shall we say, known to us at the station, so I hope you can run fast. If anybody, and I'm not saying it was you, was in his daughter's bedroom then whoever it was had better keep well clear of Mr Brennan. OK?" I nodded. I thought about the size of the shadow that I had seen in the doorway and shuddered.

So, I concluded. I definitely hadn't been called in to talk about moving into the first team squad, then.

The interview seemed to be over and Mr Busby promised the Sergeant that the club would settle any claims and thanked him. The head-coach opened the door for the officer and the secretary quickly detached herself from Georgie, who was presumably filling in some time whilst waiting for me. She handed the Sergeant a most welcome envelope and I heard the coach whisper "Good seats." and the Sergeant grinned.

The office door closed and there was silence. Mr Busby sat behind his chair and I could hear the breathing of the head coach from behind me.

Eventually Mr Busby spoke. "I think it's time for you to go home to Leeds."

That's it. I thought. It's all over. It had been good but I had blown it. That was the end of my football career. My eyes filled up. I wondered - would begging help? Where was Mum when I needed her? I was about to fall to my knees to cry for another chance when he continued.

"You've been sold to Leeds United. They are expecting you there for a medical tomorrow morning." He offered his hand, which of course I took gratefully. "Good luck. You'd better be on your way."

The head coach added "There is no time for goodbyes. I've seen that Brennan fellow and if I were you I'd get the early train. Doris has your wages. So thank you for your time at United." And that was that. After two years I was out, but at least I was still in football. Doris, the secretary, handed me an envelope with my wages in it. There was a small bonus to tide me over. Georgie, however, was distraught. He couldn't believe I was leaving. I was his best friend. I'd helped him to fit in. He'd be lonely without me – but not too lonely I thought if Doris and Jackie were anything to go by. We shook hands and I left. Georgie stayed behind because Doris had discovered that there were "Some things that she needed Georgie to go over before he went."

I stepped outside the room and there was Bobby Charlton. He was looking in a mirror and combing his hair from the side and over his pate. This was probably my last chance to speak to the great man "Mr Charlton" I said, timidly. He had a quiet presence that commanded respect. "I'm Harry Barker. I've just been sold to Leeds so I'll be joining your brother's club. I shall be there tomorrow. Do you have a message for him?"

Bobby thought a while and then, after due consideration and another glance in the mirror, he said "No."

I left the ground through a turnstile entrance. Not because I wanted to leave in shame. Oh no! I would have much preferred to take the opportunity to burst into the apprentices changing room and tell them all how Leeds had begged me to come to help save them from relegation. They weren't doing particularly well that season having lost possibly the best player in the world – John Charles - and with a new manager. Yes, I could have told quite a tale. But, no, I chose to leave quickly and without a fuss because there was already sufficient commotion at the main gates. Brennan, clearly noticeable by his size, his black Donkey Jacket and the two uniformed security guards hanging on each arm was bellowing threats and vile accusations against me.

Brave lads those security guards. "Stand fast boys" I thought and I'll have enough time to pack a suitcase and make it to the station before this man-mountain caught up with me. It was definitely time for me to make the trip back over the Pennines.

Incidentally some year's later I was given a copy of the local newspaper report. I understand the Beast is still at large.

Beast of old Trafford Hunted

Late on Saturday evening Police were called to the family home of Mr and Miss Brennan in Royston Road, Old Trafford. PC Nicholas Lightly was called to the scene by a neighbour who had interrupted a burglary in progress. Without regard for his own safety the police officer effected a rescue of Miss Brennan, who had been trapped in her bedroom by her evil assailant, as the monster leapt from an upstairs window in order to escape justice.

The "Beast of Old Trafford" was chased from the scene by an angry mob of local concerned residents who were so incensed by the horrible crime perpetrated on their doorsteps that damage was caused to a local off-license and goods to the value of £350 were stolen. Over twenty policemen quickly arrived to help quell the enraged public spirited citizens and to investigate the thefts.

Neither Mr Brennan, a widower, nor his young daughter, Doreen, were available for comment, yesterday. The curtains were closed on the upstairs window where Miss Brennan was recovering from her terrible ordeal.

A neighbour, Miss Daphne O'Flynn, 65, who caught sight of the Beast said "We are all terrified to sleep in our beds. This monster must be caught otherwise no woman will be safe. He was huge and the way he leapt from that top floor window he was like the monster out of Jekyll and Hyde. I am terrified to go home now because I live all alone at number 97."

Damage, estimated at £15 was also caused to the outside lavatory.

In a typical example of the abuse of police powers a journalist was later arrested and detained overnight for asking if the police had anything to go on.

In a separate but related incident a police inspector who had been called to the scene from a private party was involved in a serious motor vehicle accident as he drove to the scene of the attack. The Inspector's own car and a lamp post suffered significant damage when the Inspector swerved to avoid a pedestrian who had stepped into the road ahead of him. The Police Inspector, luckily, had suffered just some minor bruising however he has been suspended from duty pending an investigation into his medical condition at the time of the accident. A local resident said "He was as drunk as a Lord."

Back Home

The back streets of Leeds differed only slightly from those in Manchester. Small houses tightly packed into terraces, kids kicking battered tin cans in the streets whilst dreaming of being a world-class footballer. They called out the name of their heroes as they scored magnificent goals which struck the back of imaginary nets in front of massive crowds. The absent crowds bellowed their names in a muted roar stifled at the back of their youthful throats. Alternately they would combine their footballing skills with the role of the fawning radio commentator carelessly seeding the air with an unending supply of rich superlatives "It's Arkwright" they'd cry "Superb!" as the tin football leapt 10 yards and deflected off the inside of the lamp post to clatter across the non-existent line. Arms raised they arc a run to receive the applause of twenty thousand missing home fans while imagining how the away supporters, invariably from the much hated Arsenal, hold their head in their hands and wonder why their idiot manager failed to sign Arkwright while he was still a ten-year old. Much has changed in the last sixty years but whether it is a tin-can or a computer game the dreams are still the same. Small boys dream of being professional footballers. What do professional footballers dream of? If I remember rightly at the time it would have been Marilyn Monroe.

It was good to see Mum. Dad was away again but Uncle Vic, still at West Brom, was staying over. I moved into digs near the ground the following day. Uncle Vic was kind enough to give me a few tips on upcoming matches. I didn't place a bet. I have never been keen on gambling but I did notice that Uncle Vic was pretty good at predicting results. His predictions invariably paid off.

My first morning at Leeds United was a bit of a shock. The atmosphere at this losing club was completely different to that at Manchester United. There was a new, young manager. The older players called him Don, to his face. They didn't seem to respect him and I soon learned why. He had bought me as a centre-forward! When I explained that I was a centre-back and hadn't played up front since I was seven years old he was quite shocked and said something quite unrepeatable about the management at Manchester United. I say unrepeatable but actually over the last fifty years I have heard the very same words used by a great number of people in describing the Manchester United management. It seems that whilst their personnel may change the opinion doesn't.

Don explained that he needed a first team player and already had a very capable centre-back. I knew that – his name was Jackie Charlton. So I asked him – "Couldn't you play with two centre-backs?" He laughed. Madness he called it. How could anybody expect to win games with two centre-backs? "You have to score goals to win games, Laddie!" he cried.

"It's useless scoring three if you are letting four in" I muttered but he pretended not to hear me.

Don decided that we needed to give things a try so a practise match was arranged and I played up front. When I say "I played" I mean I stood near the opposition goal and chased after the ball when it came near. I was always in the wrong place at the wrong time and when the ball was crossed over in the air there was this giraffe of a man (Jackie) there to head it away. I was hopeless and Jackie wasted no time in telling everybody that he could do better himself. "If that's the case" says I, nearly in tears I should add. "Why don't you try it?"

"Alright." said Don "You." (He meant me, and I could tell he was not impressed.) "Swap with Jackie."

And, surprise, surprise, Jackie was not only a better centre-back than me he was also a better centre-forward. He scored within a couple of minutes, beating me to a header, elbowing me in the ribs and questioning my parentage - all in the same move. That man was a real professional.

Now I don't want to take the credit for something that I didn't do but I want to remind you here and now that it WAS my idea. Playing up front Jackie went on to score nine league goals in the final games of the season, saving Leeds from relegation and providing the platform from which Don Revie took Leeds United to their glory years and for him to become England manager. I ask nothing from you but a single word of thanks.

Isn't it funny how one thing leads to another? You may remember how, during my time in Manchester, I became known as a bit of a firebrand, a sort of footballing Mr Fix-it who was full of good ideas and the man to turn to in times of trouble. I never discouraged that misunderstanding. It suited me to have people's respect, even if it was undeserved, however in my second season with Leeds this reputation got me into some serious bother which, if it hadn't been for my quick wits and desire for survival, could have proved near fatal.

Part of the problem was that footballers of the time trained just for three or four mornings each week and even then by noon we were finished. Now it wouldn't be true to say that all the footballers then went off to sleep with other men's wives and daughters, or to the bookies to lose their "easy-gotten" on three legged nags or to the pub to waste it on cheap booze, and sometimes cheap women. Some footballers did none of this, but I have to admit most did it all. And of course this kind of behaviour led to problems.

My particular pleasure was to go to the Barnston Snooker Hall. It was a grubby place with a dozen or so snooker-tables in an underground crypt. The manager was called Swift Barry, so named from his tendency to snatch notes from the punters hands and quickly hide them within his till as if public sight of paper money may cause uproar, or, as he explained, for a thief to snatch it away. Come to think of it he was probably right. The hall was only a short walk from the training ground and the beer was palatable and competitively priced. By that I mean it was the same price as all the other ramshackle boozers in the area but the hall bar had the advantage of giving the punters something to do whilst they were drinking themselves stupid i.e. snooker.

Snooker is a fine game, played by gentlemen, which encourages fair play and honesty - in some parts of Britain. In Leeds it encouraged heavy betting and ready made weapons in the form of the six-foot spear or cudgel (also known as a cue) and the hardest balls you could hope to lay your hands on in a fight. When clenched in a fist the balls are handy for either striking your foe around the head or, as a distance weapon, they can be thrown at speeds of up to 80 miles an hour at your opponent. A bent arm IS allowed in THIS sport. When I first arrived I fell into the common trap. I won my first three games and a little cash against one of the locals, but then my luck ran out and before I knew it I was £2 down. Luckily for me I recognised early that I was being conned and accepted my losses. Others were not so lucky and one young apprentice, Dennis was his name, soon found himself with a serious debt; and to the wrong people.

One of the senior players came across Dennis moping in the changing rooms. He had been a bit of a bright spark when he arrived, all blonde hair, pace and enthusiasm but over the last few weeks he had lost his sparkle. The older player heard Dennis's story and suggested that he have a word with me to see if I could sort something out for him. So, as I was leaving for the snooker hall after training one Tuesday Dennis approached me, his sweet little face pleading, his eyes welling with tears, his hands wringing. He was pathetic and you may wonder why I gave him the time of day. Well I'll tell you. It made me feel good to have this pitiful specimen look up to me. It gave me a feeling of superiority and power and I liked that. I still like it today.

Well of course there was nothing I could do for him. I wasn't going to bail him out (even if I had the money, which I didn't). But I was in no hurry to let him know. I wanted to enjoy the moment. We walked to the snooker hall together. He had to go there to explain why he hadn't come up with the money that he owed. I was meeting some of the team there, and wanted to see what happened to Dennis. On reflection this was ill-advised. As Dennis and I entered the snooker hall three aggressive looking characters approached and surrounded us. One short, burly character, dressed in an ill-fitting black suit stood in front of us. Two larger gentlemen also suited and clearly with pugilistic experience stood at our shoulders. I tried to move past. This business had nothing to do with me but as I stepped to my left Shorty grabbed my arm and moved into my path.

"Where are you going, you long streak of piss?" He inquired disregarding the fact that we had not been formally introduced and with, if I may say without appearing standoffish, inappropriate over-familiarity.

Now you might think that with my size I should have knocked this peasant from my path with a cuff from the back of my hand and a statement to the effect of "Unhand me, you varlet!" but then it wasn't your arm he had grabbed hold of and it wasn't you who was fully focused on retaining the content of your bowels.

"So," he continued, addressing Dennis. "You've brought your big mate along to look after you, have you?"

He had got the situation completely wrong and I was just about to explain the facts to him when the cavalry arrived. Not literally you understand. It was neither a curly-haired General Custer, played by Errol Flynn, gallantly galloping into the foreground nor Robert what's-his-name leading The Knights Of The Round Table. It was in fact Jack and half a dozen of the lads who had clearly had a few on the way to the hall tumbling down the stairs and into the back of our merry group. There was a lot of "Sorry Lads" and boisterousness and by the time it was all sorted out Shorty and his two friends had decided to take their leave and had made their way up the stairs. Dennis and I looked up at them equally filled, I should think, with relief but my elation disappeared when Shorty turned at the top of the stairs and called back "I'll be seeing you, lads." Not, I thought, if I see you first.

Dennis was so pleased to have escaped from the heavies that he almost bought a round of drinks. That is he would have done except, as he explained, he was skint. He did, however, tell the lads what a great bloke I was and how I had just stood up to those three hard-men and how the three of them had been lucky that I hadn't turned nasty. And I let him talk. After all it'd be wrong to call the fellow a liar but I decided that the next time I saw Shorty I'd be quick to tell him that he'd got the wrong man.

I popped back to see Mum that evening and she passed on some information from Uncle Vic. It seemed there were a couple of games at the weekend for which the result was a fore-gone conclusion. Well worth a serious bet, Mum said. I was tempted but, like I said, gambling wasn't really my thing. She also mentioned that a fellow had been asking after me. A big chap, not local she said. I wondered who it could be but thought little more about it as I took my leave.

It was on the way back to my digs from Mum's that I came across another apprentice with a problem. Young Charlie Pascoe was saying goodbye to a petite girl outside the door of a small terraced house. When the light came on in the passageway and the front door began to open Charlie gave her a quick peck on the cheek and turned to depart. Unfortunately he turned into my path and we collided, both falling to the floor. The front door opened (immediately onto the street) and looking up from the floor I saw a short, balding, worried looking middle-aged man in the doorway and then the swollen eyes and tears that rolled down on the cheeks of the pretty young girl.

Charlie was up in a flash and recognising me he pulled me to my feet and dragged me away "Sorry, Mate. Come on. Let's go."

I've never been one to hang around where there may be trouble so I raced after him hearing the girl's father, for that was who he was, call out "'ere, 'ang on! I want a word with you." Clearly he wasn't going to get one. Not that day anyway.

I am sure you are as intrigued as I was to find out the cause of this episode so, once we had put enough distance between ourselves and the Lord of that particular Englishman's castle we stopped for a pint and young Charlie told me all about it.

Now Charlie was just nineteen, a fresh-faced honest looking lad, very much a butter-wouldn't-melt-in-his-mouth sort of a fellow. However whilst butter wouldn't melt in his mouth his girlfriend, Lucy (the aforementioned tearful lass), had melted in his arms so much that she found herself, at just seventeen, three months pregnant. Now if I had been the unwilling father I would have been on the next train out of town but young Charlie was different. I gave him my best advice but the poor little fellow was shocked at my suggestion that he deserted little Lucy. It seemed that he loved her and, if he could, he'd like to make an honest woman of the girl. Now it was my turn to be shocked. This young lad had obviously come from the far distant planet of "Fair-Play" where a society based on the principles of "Honesty" and "Virtue" produced upright citizens and sent missionaries to distant places and peoples to teach them the ways of righteousness and good-fellowship. In this specific case to me, in Leeds. I concluded this young man would have no future in football and, having suffered his pleas for help, I promised I'd think about his problem and see if I could help. His problem was, by the way, not the girl's father but the fact that on an apprentice's wage he could not afford to marry the girl let alone bring up a child.

Having shared the burden of his problems with me Charlie made his way back to his digs whilst I returned to mine, carrying the weight of his troubles plus those of Dennis. I marvelled at the stupidity of these young men as I placed my head upon my pillow that night. I lay awake, eyes open, staring at the ceiling which reflected the glow from a nearby street lamp. "What could I do to help them?" I pondered.

"Not a lot" my inner-self replied and I turned over and fell into the deep untroubled sleep of one who really couldn't give a rat's arse. Circumstances change, however.

I can't remember how it came about but the following day I found myself speaking to the manager about Charlie's dilemma. In those days a pregnant girl was considered a scandal and the football club was always keen to avoid being associated with such things. They expected their players to set an example and as a lot of football clubs were started by the local churches there remained, in those days, a link with religion. Well, when I explained that Charlie wanted to marry the girl the club and the club chaplain, who somehow had got involved, were very keen. They started a collection to help pay for a wedding and I was asked to collect from the players and to ask the local PFA representative for a contribution.

I had a bit of a problem with the PFA rep. He was due for re-election and so was visiting the club, but there was little in the Player's fund for him to contribute. Just for devilment I made a big fuss and demanded, in front of a group of other players, that he sort something out. Eventually, and reluctantly, he did. Within a couple of days, with contributions from the PFA, the club and a whip round amongst the players I had collected quite a tidy sum for the soon to be happy couple, around £100. Not a lot by today's standards but in those days that would pay for the wedding and a few things for the baby. I stowed it safely in my jacket pocket and set off for home. I didn't like to carry such a large amount of money and if it wasn't for the fact that I had a particular thirst on me at the time I would not have popped into the snooker hall as I passed for a quick drink. I did not notice the black limousine parked on the street opposite the entrance which led to the staircase down to the hall. Once inside I immediately realised my mistake. There, sitting at the bar was Shorty. He saw me enter and nodded to his two associates. They blocked off my retreat, by positioning themselves behind me at the bottom of the stairs.

"I want a word with you" smiled Shorty, leaving his barstool and walking threateningly towards me. His henchmen closed in on me, each taking an arm.

"Now hold on." I pleaded "It's not me you want. It's Dennis. I'll tell you where to find him." Well let's face it I may as well tell them now, they'd have got it out of me eventually.

"Well, if you know where Dennis is then you can give him a little message for us." Shorty explained as he brought his face up to mine, well nearly, after all I was a good eight inches taller than him. I had a nasty feeling the message was more likely to be written on my face than on a piece of paper.

"What's this?" one of the goons exclaimed, reaching into my jacket pocket and pulling out the envelope containing Charlie's collection money.

He passed the envelope to Shorty who smiled as he flicked through the notes.

"Now this is just what we've been looking for. Your chum," he meant Dennis who I assure you, as of a few moments earlier I considered to be no friend of mine and, given the opportunity, I would have gladly explained the misunderstanding to Shorty who continued to speak regardless of the inaccuracy of his assumption "owes us sixty quid. This lot here will cover it plus interest. Now I think, Mitch and Mike, you should take the lad outside and put him straight on how things work around here."

He went to pocket the money while Mitch and Mike (at last I could put a name to their brutal faces) tightened their grip on me. I didn't suppose it would have helped the situation to explain that having been brought up locally I already had a pretty fair idea on how things worked around these parts and that no further education would be necessary. I tried though. But as they began to drag me away the door at the top of the stairs opened. I looked up hopefully anticipating the arrival, once again, of my rescuers only to be stunned by the appearance at the top of the stairs of the man-mountain form of Brennan, donkey jacket and all, looking down at me with a triumphant look.

"There you are." He said as he descended towards our group. His fists clenched and unclenched in morbid anticipation.

"Hold on" said Shorty. "We've some business with this lad."

"And so have I" growled Brennan as he reached out to grab my collar.

Now it may be one of those "honour amongst thieves" or gangster's pact things but it seemed that by interfering with Mitch and Mike's planned schooling Mr Brennan had broken some sort of code of behaviour and caused some offence. The pair released me to engage with Brennan - who was equally upset that, having me at once within his grasp, these hoodlums had intervened. In short they set about each other, and whilst Mitch and Mike were no doubt very professional in their work Brennan was powerful and with the added advantage of a broken snooker cue (broken, I may add, across Mitch's back) he was more than holding his own. Shorty mistakenly felt the need to join the melee and was knocked senseless by a massive haymaker. I saw my opportunity and grabbed Charlie's money from inside Shorty's jacket and as I made my way, hastily, up the stairs tucked it safely away back into my own jacket pocket. Brennan, Mitch and Mike wrestled with grunts, groans and understandably coarse language in a pile around Shorty. Exit, promptly, one relieved young man.

Of course my luck couldn't hold. As I backed out of the snooker hall door onto the street a hand was placed upon my shoulder. There, in a very smart chauffer's uniform was the ugliest man I have ever seen. The flesh around his eyes was covered with scar tissue and his nose looked as if it had been spread across his face with a spade. Incidentally I learned later that this was because his nose had actually been spread across his face by a spade but that wasn't important. This man stood a good three inches taller than me and he wasn't smiling. A darkened window on the limousine rolled down and a man's voice gently asked if I would like to get into the car. I pondered the question briefly but one look at Lurch in his chauffeur's cap convinced me the right answer was "Yes". So, with the car door being opened for me, I stepped into the back seat which was offered. Lurch closed the door and returned to the driver's seat.

"Can I give you a lift somewhere?" asked my host, a hard looking man in his thirties who wore a very expensive dark suit and narrow black tie. He smelled of perfume, which gave me some doubts, but his confident air convinced me that that the suggestion was not optional.

I considered his offer and looked back out of the car door window, considering my chances should I jump out and run for it. At that moment the decision was made for me. Brennan appeared at the doorway of the snooker hall. Were it not for the torn shoulder of his jacket, the blood pouring from a wound in the side of his head and the snapped snooker cue held like a claymore in his left hand one would not have thought he had been in a fight. Fortunately Brennan could not see through the darkened windows of the limousine; but he was uncomfortably close.

"Yes," I replied to my big-hearted rescuer "that'd be nice. Could you take me home, please?"

"And where would that be?" he asked. And I lied, of course.

I can't remember the full content of the conversation with my wealthy benefactor but it transpired that Shorty and the boys worked for let's (for the sake of everybody's future health and safety) call him, Mr A. He may have been dead these last twenty years but then again, he may not.

Mr A. had a concern that if people got into the habit of not paying their gambling debts then that would make his job, which was to keep order, very difficult and that he would then have to work even harder to keep his business in profit. He asked if I understood, and I did. It was important, he explained, that people like Dennis pay their debts. I agreed with him and he was pleased and wondered if I could help him find a solution to a little problem that he had. We agreed that Dennis owed him some money and that had to be paid. We also agreed that Dennis had not shown sufficient respect to Mr A. and that was unacceptable and further Mr A. had needed to invest his time and his operative's time (he meant Shorty, Mitch and Mike. Keep up!) and for that he needed compensation. Dennis, he explained, wasn't there. However I was. So how could I help him to resolve this very regrettable state of affairs?

Good question, I thought. More importantly, how can I get out of this car in one piece and then get out of this town? It was suddenly very hot in the car. I felt a trickle of sweat drip from my forehead onto my cheek. Mr A. was looking at me. He was smiling. He was sure that I could think of something but the only thing I could think of is what Mum would think when the police came to her door to tell her a body had been found. Mum! Where was she when I needed her? Mummy! Oh God, Mummy! I may have been about to start wailing and crying for her when something deep in my subconscious triggered a thought. Mum! That was the answer. Uncle Vic.

And so the deal was done. Mr A. dropped me at Don's house (I'll not have him track me back to my digs) and I waved him goodbye – then set off on the three mile walk home.

After the weekend football results came in there were cheers all round. I placed the whole of Charlie's collection money on the unlikely results that Uncle Vic had told Mum about. That gave Charlie enough to pay for the wedding and a good deposit to put down on a little tobacconist shop near the ground. He'd never make it as a footballer. Too honest I suppose. Dennis had put his week's wages and every penny he could find on the games and now had enough to pay Mr A. what was owed and as for me, well I made a few bob but more importantly when I left the snooker hall on Sunday afternoon Mr A. was waiting for me in his car. He had bet a four figure sum and made a solid fortune. He and the boys were just off to collect it. From now on I was protected, which was lucky because Shorty, Mitch and Brian were carrying some nasty looking cuts and bruises. Mr A. dropped me off "at home", again, and worryingly promised to be in touch.

Excellent, I thought, and as the rain started to fall I once again began the three mile hike.

The PFA Again

Word gets around, of course, and the way that Dennis and Charlie's problems were resolved became folklore among the local players. Of course they didn't know the detail of how I managed to come up with the answers or the results and I am not sure I knew all the details myself. "Ask me no questions and I'll tell you no lies" they say and whilst that may strictly be true I am not saying that an unsolicited lie won't slip from my tongue occasionally. It may surprise you to learn that I do not pretend to be a saint.

As I mentioned earlier the PFA representative election was due and our Rep had been keen to stand. However the way I had berated his lack of effort in providing some support for Charlie when it was needed and the way the team had joined me in giving him a hard time led him to declare that we could all get stuffed if we thought he'd perform the thankless task for another year and if they wanted that big bag of shite (he may possibly have meant me) to represent them then as far as he was concerned the whole lot of them could stick the job up their collective arses. The general consensus was that somebody had upset him. Anyway the job paid a couple of quid a week and I could always use the extra so when the boys decided to put me up for election I was not going to say "No". So, I didn't, and God bless me if I wasn't duly elected (unopposed) as the PFA Rep for the district. Mum would be so proud. One thing that I hadn't realised was that in my new capacity I would have to go to London and Manchester, on expenses paid trips, every few months and that I'd be meeting with my old friend, Jimmy the Chin, when I got there. I wondered if he would remember me.

Now one of the things that any new manager wants to do is to give the impression to the Football Club Directors that he is going to be very careful with their money. They are a funny old lot the Directors of Football Clubs. Nowadays you're talking about Russian billionaires with a yacht the size of a battleship and trophy wives hanging on their arms who'd have most Miss Worlds crying over their relatively flat chests and reaching for the spot cream and dieting book. But in those days it was your local ruddy faced butcher or newsagent who'd turn up in his works van not so much with a trophy wife more a case of getting out of the house for a few hours to get away from the old girl. Their one aim in life would be to live out their unrequited footballing fantasies through the likes of myself.

I reckon that seeing players receiving applause and cheers from the supporters each week must have really grated with the directors and as a result they liked nothing more than to be quoted in the local rag saying how certain players needed to "buck up their ideas" or they'd be sold on, or alternately how smart they, the directors, were to find the players that were doing so well. Players were contracted to clubs and, long before Bosman, if a club decided a player was going to Timbuktu or the bottom club in the Third Division North or even worse, North Wales, then that's where he went. No choice. Uproot your family or leave them behind if you want, just go. I suppose having that power made the directors feel better about themselves. A bit like medieval kings, and usually just about as popular – and I am thinking more King John than Richard the Lion-heart. So what it came to for me was that Don soon realised that Manchester United had sold him a pup, or a donkey, or a cart-horse or any other semi-domesticated animal that you would like to describe me as. In the close season before my first full season started at Leeds I was played in a few "friendlies" to give me a chance to show what I could do. Once Don had seen what I could do he realised it wasn't what he, or anybody else for that matter, wanted. There had been talk of Jackie going to join his brother at Manchester United but Don managed to stop that. I think that if I had shown any kind of ability or potential then Jackie would have been off. I don't think Jackie ever really forgave me for that. It's not that he was unhappy at Leeds but the money at United was very attractive and Jackie had spent enough time in Yorkshire to know the value of a penny, or in Jackie's case, a half-penny.

So for the start of the new season Jackie was back at centre-half and I was in the reserves. Well, over the next season or so I got an occasional game when there were injuries but nobody, including me, expected much more. To their credit the fans were not unkind to me. I have heard groans arise from some supporters when unpopular players haven take the field. I'm not sure how a player must feel when his name is called out by an apologetic megaphone announcer - as if he too can't believe that this cart-horse is being given ANOTHER chance, and then the groan from the crowd, a buzz of conversation with the word "wanker" most prominent. This topped by a small child who starts to cry and ask his dad if they can go home. Fortunately that never happened to me but I've seen other players visibly wilt on entering the pitch to that kind of welcome. Was it any surprise that their first tentative touch of the ball would put the opposition in with a chance thus confirming everybody's prejudiced opinion? Anyway the crowd at Leeds sort of liked me. I knew I had to keep it simple so, true to form, I stayed back and when anything came near me I kicked it. It seemed to work and sometimes if I was lucky I'd kick something solid and we'd be playing against ten men. No substitutes for injured players in those days. They liked that at Elland Road especially against the southern softies; and the referees, presumably, couldn't afford eyesight tests.

So although Don knew I'd not make it as a first team player he wasn't quite ready to go to the board and say "You remember that fellow I asked to buy last year? Well he's rubbish so can I have some more of your ill-gotten to buy someone else, ta very much?" No, Don wasn't that daft. By the way I haven't mentioned what my transfer fee from Manchester United was, not because I am too embarrassed but because I have never been told. I wasn't the sort of player whose transfer was going to make back page news, let alone front page news. It did get a two line mention in the local press as an example of how the club lacked ambition and were scraping the barrel for bigger club's cast-offs. My first mention in the press - but I didn't bother keeping the cutting for my scrapbook. As for a signing-on fee, I remember one of the backroom staff sidling up to me at the end of training a few days after I had joined the club. He looked carefully from side-to-side over each of his shoulders like a soon to be exterminated character from a Harry Palmer spy movie and then forcefully pressed a nice crisp fiver into my palm. Being a well brought up lad I checked over both my own shoulders and slipped the note into my pocket. In my time that kind of thing was called "a drink". Nowadays it'd be called a "financial irregularity" and would require the services of a High Court judge, two Briefs costing more per day than most people earn in a month and all the journalists, sober or otherwise, that "Fleet Street" can muster to try to pin the case on some hapless manager who has only been doing what everybody else has been doing for years - but have been better at hiding. Progress they call it! Still I shan't complain because while the authorities are putting on a show trial in order to pin a misdemeanour on "Ron Manager" and his like all the really worthwhile scams, the all-expenses paid trips to far-flung islands "to promote England's bid" and the back-handers paid to match officials to ensure the right results go by un-investigated. It's not like that abroad, you know. Look at Germany - some people have ended up in prison just because a few results have become known before the games have started! There are two sides to German efficiency. They can keep their World Cups — I'd rather sleep sound in my bed. But it wasn't always swept under the carpet over here. I came rather close myself on one occasion.

Mind you I couldn't get a drink in my club for a fiver now. Don't worry I'm not going to drone on about how for less than half a crown (twelve and a half new pence, I mean.) I could get three pints, three gin and tonics and a fish and chip supper for me and a close friend every night for a month. But that's not what I would have spent my money on. Three pints, sure. Gin and tonic, fair enough. I know you've heard it all before from your granddad. But, by spending a fiver in London I could usually find myself performing a close investigation of the contents of some pretty fancy underwear belonging to one of the girls from the Gaslight Club, late at night in a cosy nook in the West End. Good times those and not a penny was wasted.

In the early sixties London was the place to be, and it was getting better. It got a bit serious later in the decade when the gangsters got involved but at first it was fun, fun, fun. Money was flowing freely. The post-war generation were gearing up to really let their hair down and the women weren't waiting for Germaine Greer to tell them they could enjoy themselves. They hadn't read Lady Chatterley's Lover and they didn't need to whilst me and the lads were there to take 'em to the potting shed, so to speak. They wanted to enjoy themselves and I was quite happy to help 'em get the most out of life. And I wasn't the only young, fit footballer who was prepared to put in some extra effort. The clubs were full of us and it was all there. Women. Gambling. Drinking. Women. And then the same thing all over again but, for a bit of variety, in a different order.

It wasn't just us footballers though. There was a kind of pecking order. We were somewhere near the bottom of a pile that was headed up by the actors and pop musicians. They got first choice — after Royalty of course. Then there were the politicians, you had to watch them though because you never knew where their fancies would take them. We footballers and the boxers came next followed by the other sportsmen and bottom of the heap were the producers, artists and writers and the like. I think the girls gave them attention only because they thought they could introduce them to the actors.

Early in sixty-one I was doing very nicely with a stunning red-head in a club called Murrays. She'd been introduced to me, kind of, by my osteopath, Stephen. He'd been doing some work in his clinic on my back. I had managed to arrange for the PFA to pay for this expensive treatment every time I was in London, one of the benefits of the job I suppose. When I saw him in the club with this stunner I didn't hesitate to go over and introduce myself. Taking the girl away from him would be an opportunity to get even with him for some of the agony he had caused me when working on the muscles in my lower back. Stephen didn't seem to mind my interruption and went off to speak to one of the politicians; an expensively suited middle-aged gent. That suited me just fine. Christine, that was her name, flirted with me outrageously. There were fleeting touches on my upper arm and outer thigh. To put it "romantically" I, and my underpants, were quickly filled with desire but I noticed that her big eyes which were heavily made up with black mascara occasionally looked over to where Stephen spoke with his friend. In his line of work Stephen maintained a muscular physique but he didn't have my good looks and, by the natural order of things, girls would never pick a mere medical man over a professional sportsman. I mean he wasn't even a plastic surgeon or somebody who could perform a heart transplant, he just moved meat and bones about. Like a butcher but without the blood.

Never in my life had I met such a desirable woman. Her skin was perfect, her figure sublime. If Helen of Troy looked half as good, and I assure you she didn't, then it was no wonder the world went to war for her. I was just about to suggest that we leave for somewhere more private when I noticed her eyes had once again moved to where Stephen and his friend were now approaching us. Her gorgeous lips parted as her perfect teeth were suddenly exposed in the broadest of smiles, her hand extended towards Stephen's companion. He took her hand and their eyes met. My heart, followed by my erection, sank.

"This," said Stephen, performing the introduction, "is John. He's in Government."

"How interesting!" replied Christine "You must tell me all about it."

I whimpered. She hadn't looked at me like that. It was a look which I could best describe as devouring. John was a delicious cream cake and she was about to nibble away at him until he was all gone and John was going to enjoy every moment of it. He leaned towards her and whatever he said made her laugh beautifully. With a short glance towards me the pair moved away towards the dance-floor. I was dismissed and I didn't like it one bit. I moved forward but Stephen was blocking my path.

"I really need to talk to you about your back. I noticed that when you were speaking to Christine you were leaning forward a lot." Of course I bloody-well was! I hoped he wasn't expecting to get paid for this consultancy.

I looked over his head to where Christine was moving sensuously against John on the dance-floor. I whimpered again.

Stephen managed to draw my eyes away for an instant and with a firm grip on my arm quietly explained.

"Harry, she's out of your price-range."

I looked down at him, quizzically. Then, once again, at her on the dance-floor. I may have reminded a casual onlooker of a child looking at an unattainable tasty treat through a shop window.

Stephen shook his head from side to side. "No, Harry." He calmly confirmed that she was lost to me and like a mother leading her child from a sweet-shop window he guided me away and back to the bar for a consolation drink. In that moment I hated that politician and although I was never, well rarely, one to seek retribution in this case I wanted to make an exception. He'd never get my vote I decided with a pout that any thirteen year old girl would have been proud of!

Back to football, though. It was a lot easier for Don to let me troll along, playing every now and then and drawing a small wage. I didn't mind because I had found other interests. There was a lot of activity in the PFA so my trips were becoming more frequent, and more enjoyable. What had happened was that after the abolition of the maximum wage the players had come to realise that they could get what they wanted. And they wanted plenty so, more and more, I found myself on the train down to London with my suitcase packed for a two night stay.

I don't want you to think that we did nothing on these trips. The lads were putting together a fine bunch of proposals and I'd done my bit to help pull them together. Not that I put a lot of hard work in myself. I did most of my work in what you might call "the field". That is I'd spend time with the players asking them what they thought we should do. They wanted more money, of course, but they also wanted something done about how they could be sold on without their agreement and half a dozen other things.

Well I would listen to all this airy-fairy stuff and buy another round of drinks (on expenses, mind) and the lads thought I was a great bloke and I told 'em that I'd see what I could do. I could have told them right there and then that they had no chance but then why spoil a good night out? Sure I'd go back to the PFA committee and tell them how the players were demanding this and that and the committee would all nod their heads in agreement, encouraging me along and I'd speak louder and louder and get a round of applause and numerous slaps on the back. Then it'd be time for dinner, and off to a club for a good night out. Nothing got done, of course, but everybody seemed to feel a lot better for this and I wasn't complaining – especially when it came to the 1962 World Cup.

Of course we all remember 1966, and I'll get to that in good time, but everybody has forgotten Chile in 1962 and the disappointment of not winning the World Cup then. You can't pin that on me, though. Well, maybe not entirely. We had a good team, I'm told, and really fancied our chances. Chile is a long way away and opportunities to travel abroad were pretty limited in those days so there were quite a few of us in the PFA who felt the need to travel with the lads – in order to protect their interests, you understand. Expenses paid! South America! Castanets and Latin women! You can bet there was a lot of interest. The problem I had was how to make sure that I got the job. The chairman was the most likely candidate and he was pretty confident going into the meeting where we'd pick "Our Man". Of course he had a good case. He was the chairman after all.

But we managed to persuade him, with a vote of 24-1, that he was needed back home formulating our forthcoming proposal to the F.A. for better working conditions for the players.

As you see only one person voted in favour of the chairman going. That, of course, was me. Confused? Yes I know I said I wanted to go myself but this is how it works.

The chairman desperately wanted to go. He'd even been out to buy himself a pair of khaki shorts and some sun-tan oil. So just before the meeting where we were going to pick "Our Man for Chile" I promised him my support, nice and loud so everybody could hear it. Then, as the meeting began, I stood up and made the speech of my life.

Firstly I told the gathering how important it was that the chairman should represent us at this auspicious international event. I then told 'em that we shouldn't spend a lot of time talking about who should be going because the most important thing on our agenda should be the rights of our members, the players! I then got myself, apparently, all worked up. Throwing my huge frame up from my chair I wind-milled my arms around, emphasising every point I was making, a bit like Hitler on a bad day. (Did he have bad days? I mean, how bad could they get?) I ranted. I raved. I fell short of personal abuse although I might have implied that we'd get a lot more done if the Chairman was out of the way. I required that action be taken. I demanded that players must be allowed to sign for any club they chose. I insisted on full pay throughout the summer and a minimum wage for all players up until the national retirement age. All kit and boots were to be paid for by the clubs but players could seek sponsorship wherever they chose. Transfer fees had to be shared equally between the clubs and the players. Taxis were to be provided to take players from their homes and back again after matches and training. (That was to cut down on drink-driving offences, it made sense you see!) I even seem to remember demanding three weeks off at Christmas and a free turkey all around. And if we didn't get it? I would call for a full strike, sit-ins at the football grounds, setting up our own leagues and horse-whipping every member of the F.A. I then told the stunned group that if this committee couldn't deliver then maybe it was time for new blood. Too much time and money was spent on lunches and dinners for the committee members and it was time to give the people we represented value for their money. Younger blood (I was the youngest there by quite a few years.) was needed. Action had to be taken!

I remember their faces even now. Open mouthed and perspiring. Utter shock. They saw this young firebrand was about to upset the whole gravy-train. Radical action! Strikes! People going without pay! PFA subscriptions not paid! Problems with the FA! And who knows, the players may be prepared to follow this handsome Bonny Prince? They were speechless, dumbstruck, almost, but fortunately not quite, to a man.

Well just as soon my backside had settled back onto the leather clad chair up pops our canny representative from West London with a suggestion.

"My colleague from Yorkshire is quite right." He says. They looked at him in quiet anticipation. "Young blood is what we need, but with experience."

"And what better way" he continued, holding the full attention of the crowd "to gain that experience than with the England team in Chile. There he'll be able to keep an eye on the FA chiefs and protect our most valuable player's interests."

Well you've never heard such a clamour. There were more "Hear! Hear!"s thrown around than at a Conservative Party conference. The man from Up West was slapped on the back and received the Chairman's thanks for proposing such a good idea. The final word then came from our illustrious chairman who added that I was quite right and that we should not spend too much time debating the trip to Chile as there were more pressing matters. In fact, he suggested, if I were in agreement and the vote carried, that I should make my way right now to make my preparations to travel. I'd need a passport and expenses of course. "How" he asked, "would I feel about taking the trip on behalf of them all?"

It was important that I played my hand just right. If I showed too keen then they'd smell a rat; too slow and they may change their minds.

"But if I go" says I "what'll happen to all the ideas that I had for the player's rights?" (Did you notice how they'd now become MY ideas.) Well I was not to worry it seems. The rest of the committee were going to take them on board and do what they could to push them through. Don't worry, I was told. Go to Chile and try to take advantage of all that the experience offers. It's a once in a lifetime experience I was told. And they were right. It was!

The vote was called for and I felt it only right that I should abstain. Only fair don't you think? So after a 24-0 decision I was ushered out of the door with everybody's best wishes and set off to get my photograph taken for my passport. I paused outside as the door was closed just long enough to hear a communal sigh of relief and the chairman ask if anybody else felt like a drink. I know I did!

Chile 1962

I was as excited as a schoolboy seeing his first centrefold when I joined the official party at Heathrow. I got a fair welcome from the England squad as they recognised me as one of their own. That is to say I'd been drunk with most of them and was not shy of buying a drink. The FA Officials looked at me with suspicion though. Not the right sort of fellow they thought. "He's a communist" I think I heard one of them say. I wasn't sure what he was talking about. I'd never been to Russia and didn't fancy it much either. All that snow. Why get chilly when you can go to Chile! Alright, I never said I was a comedian.

It took us two days to get to Santiago stopping at New York and a couple of other airports on the way. By the time we arrived we'd gone through every drop of alcohol on the flight deck and even drained a pilot's hip flask. There weren't as many regulations in those days. The players were under scrutiny and expected not to drink. At first I managed to sneak a few bottles through to some of the players, it always pays to look after the right people, but after twenty-four hours of travel everybody had lost interest in everything. The FA officials were dozy. I mean dozing (there I go again with the high-octane humour) so we could do pretty much as we pleased. I passed a bottle forward to Bobby Charlton but he wasn't interested and passed it back to one of the Jimmy's sitting behind him. I can't remember if it was Greavsie or Armfield. You work it out. Later on the flight I had a good chat with the Jimmys. Good lads the pair of them but could they talk? On and on about football. Greavsie was a laugh a minute but Jimmy Armfield took it all very seriously. Play for England? He could talk for England. Sometimes when I am dozing on a Saturday afternoon I think I can still hear his voice distantly describing the action from a football match far away. It takes me back to that flight and the good times we had but I suppose that's just me as an old man, dreaming of days gone by.

You'd think we'd be too tired to do anything but sleep when we finally arrived in Chile but having checked into our second-rate hotel a few of the lads were ready to see some of the sites. Walter Winterbottom (you may recall he managed England before the great Sir Alf) wasn't keen on the lads going out for a drink so although a couple of the players were game for a quick one after a short while I found myself in unfamiliar company.

On leaving the hotel we had been guided to what was considered an exclusive haunt. It was full of dark-haired Hispanics and their gorgeous coffee-skinned girlfriends. How these short, slippery looking fellows managed to attract so many tall, shapely women I have no idea. Yes I do. They were the local money and women are the same the world over. A fellow can be an absolute pig in looks and behaviour but if he has the cash he'll find a pretty girl who is happy to share it with him. No point complaining about it, that's just how it works. I took one look at a little fellow who stood beside a stunning dark-skinned woman. She was just over five feet tall and very shapely. She had what they call "it" - that indefinable quality that few women have but which makes men fall at their feet. An "it" girl may not necessarily be a classic beauty but, fellas, when you see one you'll know what I mean. He, however, could hardly walk straight and seemed to have a bent leg. He was also worse for the drink and although any man in the place would have given his right arm (that's probably an exaggeration but I'm trying to make a point here) for five minutes with this woman (and I assure you they were all staring) she had eyes only for him.

And that's where the trouble started. There were a couple of Yanks (what were they doing anywhere near a football competition?) who were looking a bit too obviously and, once he realised, the little fellow took offence. He said something quite terse in what turned out to be Portuguese and gave them some kind of hand signal which, whilst I was unfamiliar with its precise meaning, was sufficiently clear. The Americans seemed to think that was funny and enjoyed a good laugh at the little fellow's expense right up to the point where he threw a plate of tortillas into their faces. The crowd were on the little fellow's side. They all seemed to know him and cheered as the spicy delicacy dripped from the Citizens of the United States' chins.

The woman, very strong it seems, was trying to drag the drunken dynamo away, pleading with him to leave them alone but it was too late. The Americans jumped up and advanced. They were much bigger than him and it looked to be no contest. But then I haven't survived in a thousand nightclubs without recognising when outsiders were going to get a pasting from the locals. You try going out for a drink in Glasgow with an English accent and you'll learn to keep your mouth shut. I know. I know. You can't drink with your mouth shut. Will you let me get on with the story?

Well, there I was, sitting in my booth with it all about to go off. The Yanks were up and each was holding a bottle by its neck. The crowd seemed to bristle, muscles tightened, adrenalin began to course through Anglo-Saxon and Latino veins. The woman's eyes met mine and at that moment I fell in love. Alright, lust, but if you'd seen her you wouldn't have blamed me. And I stood up. And I stepped forward. And I moved between the Americans and the happy couple. And I said quietly to the Americans, pointing to the exit.

"Lads. If you take just a moment to look around you will see that you are surrounded by about a hundred locals who will tear you to pieces if you take just another step forward. The best thing for you to do is to get out of here as quickly as you can. I'll try to hold them off but you'd better scarper!"

Now I don't think the other people in the bar could hear what I was saying, or possibly could understand English but what they saw was this tall, elegant hero stepping between two large, aggressive, tooled up bullies to protect a small man with his wonderful woman. This Sir Galahad (or whatever the Chilean equivalent is - Don Quixote maybe? Bernardo O'Higgins probably) quietly, but firmly, warns off the villains who then looking furtively around, silently put their weapons back on the beer mats and reverse out of the premises like Butch Cassidy and Sundance leaving a bank.

This wasn't quite the gamble from me that it may sound because I'd had a bit of a chat with the Yanks earlier in the evening. One of them thought I looked familiar and asked if I was a sportsman. I told him I was a footballer – which led to the usual confusion that it does with Americans – and I still didn't get an answer to which part of the word they didn't understand the "foot" bit or the "ball" bit. Anyway, on the basis that the Leeds United second string were hardly household names in Leeds let alone 3,000 miles away in the US of A we concluded that I just reminded him of somebody and left it at that.

Well once they'd left I was clearly the hero of the hour. I couldn't drink enough Pisco to satisfy my new found group of friends and although I spent the evening in the company of the little fellow and his beautiful companion I made no headway. She was only interested in him. She did, however, introduce me to a very pleasant look-alike who lived up to all my hopes and expectations – and why not? There's no point in losing sleep over the unattainable. Take what you can when you can, I say.

I woke the next morning with the sun blazing through open windows onto a well kept but well worn apartment. Alone I may add. I shuffled around and eventually my hostess, Juanita, arrived with the little fellow from the bar. It seems he had a favour to ask of me. Juanita left the room to make some fantastic coffee and I took the opportunity to ask the vital question.

"Who was that little bird you were with?"

"Little bird?" he laughed "I like that".

I didn't get the joke but when he told me what he wanted me to do I soon forgot about that. I'll cut to the chase. It seems my little friend, whose name was Manuel, was a married man. I know, I know it happens to the best of us and the worst of us. Unfortunately little Elsie (his English wasn't great so the name may have changed in translation) hadn't been his first choice as a life-partner, until recently, and I couldn't blame him for that. None of us can see round corners. He explained that with Chile and his home country, Brazil, being strict Roman Catholic countries it was a problem for a man like him and a woman like Elsie to spend too much time together.

I'm not sure what the problem with that was, our politicians were doing this kind of thing all the time and it never stopped them from drawing a very decent salary. Anyway what my new friend needed was somebody to accompany Elsie to a place called Viña Del Mar on the coast where he had some business to attend to. She'd be shacked up in a local hotel and he could come to visit her late at night, presumably disguised as a postman or something.

I asked him to repeat that and he did, so I will. He wanted me to accompany the sexiest woman I had ever seen in my life to a hotel on the coast and pretend to be her "special friend" for a few days while she waited for him to turn up occasionally for a conjugal visit.

"But what would we do with our time?" I asked (a few ideas were forming in my grubby little head.)

"Go to the beach," he suggested "Visit the bars and nightclubs. You'll have a great time. She is good fun." (I bet she is, I thought.) "She will entertain you." (I should hope so, thinks I.)

Well I gave his idea full consideration for just less than half a second before agreeing. Having arranged a meeting place he shook my hand vigorously, called me his greatest friend and hobbled away with his curious rolling gait. I wondered how this little fellow managed to pull fantastic little Elsie but I reckon that if I couldn't make some headway with her during a three or four nights stay in a hotel then I may as well chop it off and become a nun. I know it ain't all about the size of the man – I recall Mae West, when talking to a particularly tall and attractive fellow is reputed to have said "Six foot six? Never mind the six foot let's talk about the six inches." Well I was six foot four but don't let that fool you. Juanita came back in with the coffee. She was wearing a loose slip which, as she leaned over to place the small cup on the table, allowed me a full view of her excellent breasts. I took a mouthful and then proceeded to demonstrate to her how excited I was at the thought of spending a few days on the coast with Elsie.

Viña Del Mar was the resort chosen by the Brazilian football squad as their base for the World Cup so I was not surprised to see a horde of photographers waiting in the arrival lounge when Elsie and I got off the plane. They started pushing and shoving in their haste to take some snaps of Elsie. I guessed they were waiting for somebody from the Brazilian squad but on seeing little Elsie with her firm curvy legs enhanced by a short red dress which covered her, just, from her thighs to her cleavage they must have decided to grab some shots, if not for the family album then for personal use on lonely nights away from home. Elsie played up to them, striking poses and leaning a little forward to make sure they got the best shots. Once they had taken a few she grabbed my arm and cuddled up. Making it clear, to one and all, that I was the lucky fellow that would be getting a private showing later – and if things went to plan then they'd be right. I looked down to see her large brown eyes looking admiringly up into my own – what an actress! But I enjoyed it and looking around I could see the jealous eyes of the ensemble. If felt great – and so did Elsie!

The hotel was about as good as it gets in that part of Chile at that time – which, frankly, wasn't that good. Worn carpets, wicker furniture and a creaky bed covered by a tired mattress. Elsie and I booked into separate, but adjoining, rooms. We weren't married you see and although everybody knew what was going on (or thought they did) there were no shared rooms for unmarried couples. The hotel wouldn't allow it and why should they? They could charge for two rooms and only wash one set of laundry - but not for Elsie and me. We arrived late in the evening and Elsie was straight off to bed. I had a drink in the little bar where the barman continually gave me admiring glances and the widest smile his face could offer.

Elsie didn't rise till after mid-day, which suited me, and then she wanted to go shopping. Not for me, I thought, but then again maybe if I bought her a few trinkets she may feel the need to thank me in some way. So off we went walking the streets and looking in the tatty clothes shops. It was soul destroying except for the times when Elsie would ask for my opinion on a dress. That would give me the opportunity to admire her form, and she didn't seem to mind if I put a hand here and there to indicate where I thought it was a bit loose or too tight. By the time we returned to the hotel I was more than ready. Elsie disappeared into her room for a shower which gave me the opportunity to pop downstairs to collect a pre-ordered bottle of their finest plonk. Chilled, as you can imagine, to the point where you couldn't taste it at all. It was better that way.

Oh, the anticipation as I made my way back up the stairs! I'd bought her a particularly skimpy two-piece swimsuit and hoped to persuade her to try it on. Two glasses in hand I knocked carefully on her door. She opened it – already wearing the bikini and looking fantastic. Her tight stomach showed not an ounce of spare. Her legs I have already told you about and there she was smiling as broadly as I could have hoped.

"How thoughtful of you!" she exclaimed happily. "That is so kind of you. Come in."

I didn't wait to be asked twice and why should I? She was obviously already way ahead of me.

"Look" she took the wine and glasses from me and turned to the smiling man sitting upright in her bed "Harry has brought us some wine!"

My little friend, Manuel, leaped out of bed, naked as a Jay-bird and strode, shall we say man-fully, towards me. Now as a footballer you get used to men walking around with nothing on and you tend to deliberately take no notice. You certainly wouldn't want to be caught checking out the size of the opposition. It wasn't so much that it became obvious why little Elsie found him so attractive but I noticed how his right leg was so bent that it seemed to curve <u>with</u> his bowed left leg a bit like two open brackets next to each other. I may have embarrassed myself by staring and Elsie threw a towel towards him telling him to cover-up. Maybe she was embarrassed.

Manuel caught the towel and put it around his waist. He then walked over and gave me a friendly hug. Not something that I was particularly keen on, especially as he used both hands to hug me and the towel fell carelessly to the floor revealing everything again. I wished to God I hadn't automatically bent down to pick it up for him.

"But how did you know I was here?" He asked.

"Oh, I didn't" I blurted out before realising that he may then want to know what I was doing bringing wine to his girlfriend's room "but I knew you wouldn't be long because Elsie was so keen to get back to the hotel." So she had been, but not as keen as me.

There were no further questions as Elsie then raised her arms above her head like a ballerina and gracefully turning on her heels she asked "How do you like the bikini that Harry bought me?"

The answer, based on the fact that both our mouths fell open, was "a lot". Never let people tell you that hairy armpits can't be attractive. Manuel walked over, picked her up, and placed her on the bed. His towel was not going to be in place much longer so I decided to leave. There are limits, you know.

Back in my room I took a shower and had a brief nap. Not easy with the noises coming from Elsie's room. I didn't expect to see either of them that evening and was debating whether to go out and get drunk or … well that was about it really. However I was soon rescued by a timid tap on the door. The hotel clerk stood outside. The smile on his face suggested that he wanted to share some happy thoughts. In this instance it was with me. Downstairs, he explained, there were some people to see me.

"Preety people" he grinned, his eyebrows raised and lowered meaningfully.

I took the hint, dressed quickly and followed him down to reception where two girls waited.

"Are you a friend of the little bird?" the dyed blonde one asked. It's funny how a name catches on I thought.

"Sure" I said "but I am on my own at the moment." It was worth a try. Neither girl had Elsie's class but they weren't bad at all. The dyed blonde was slim with wide dark eyes whilst the natural dark brunette had a sultry, knowing look that couldn't fail. Both looked as fit as ferrets.

"The Little Bird asked us to keep you company." Blondie informed me.

"Shall we go out for a drink?" The other asked.

"Or stay in?" said Blondie, laughing as she took my arm in hers and led me to the exit and out into the warm evening air.

Well I'm not one to rush things, sometimes, and I was peckish so off we went into the town to find some "vittals" and whatever the night would bring.

I seem to recall that it brought quite a lot. It turned out that Elsie was in the entertainment business and these two beauties were both dancers. And boy, could they move! We hit the clubs and bars until the early hours. I was in good shape but these girls were in better. The booze kept flowing and I drank my fill of the local fire-water. Sure enough, the next afternoon I woke butt-naked on the bed with the mother of all hangovers. The girls had gone. I immediately checked for my wallet but it was still there. Depleted due to the night's excesses, but not empty. I struggled to bring to mind all the activity of the previous night remembering some close contact with the girls but that was all I could remember. I must have dropped off to sleep when we got back to the hotel. I could see the girls had stayed the night from the state of the bathroom and I started to remember them pulling at my clothes. The memories started to come back to me. Damn. One of the greatest experiences of my life and I could hardly remember a bloody thing. That's the evil of alcohol my friend, be warned!

Elsie and I spent the afternoon on the beach. That bikini was money well-spent and there were a hundred voyeurs who could testify to that. Rubbing oil into Elsie's bare back wasn't all I had in mind but it would have to do until a better opportunity presented itself. The beaches were fantastic and there were more golden figures strolling provocatively along those pale white sands than in any beauty pageant but Elsie had "it" and I, like so many others wanted what it was she had. Any sportsman will tell you that you must "focus". So I focussed on Elsie.

We returned to the hotel as the evening cooled but as we approached photographers appeared out of the doorways like cockroaches crawling onto walls when darkness falls. Elsie took my arm and once again we appeared like a close couple. I didn't mind as she pressed against me, smiling for the cameras. Close coupling was exactly what I had in mind but as we reached her room she let go of my arm and opened the door.

"Those photographers are a problem" she said turning to me in the doorway "Manuel will not be able to come this evening."

"Good" I thought but "that's a shame." I replied "What shall we do?" I could have made a suggestion, but didn't. Sometimes it pays to be subtle. "Perhaps we should stay in or is there somewhere I could take you?" I was being charming, you see.

Her face lit up. "Of course! Let's take a shower and then go to dinner together." I was half-way through her door before I realised that she meant separate showers followed by a meal together. I wouldn't have minded if it was the other way round even though I do like company when I am eating.

Elsie took me to what was probably the most expensive restaurant in the area. Whilst the band played Latino music they served a fantastic chilli but it didn't cost me a bean! During the meal Elsie wrote a small note and passed it, with a small denomination tip, to a waiter. She whispered to him and he gave her a knowing smile and a wink before he disappeared. I thought nothing of it at the time.

As we finished our meal the owner came to our table with a bottle of their very best imitation champagne and asked if Elsie would consider singing for his restaurant. She obliged, and I must say she was good. The crowd rose to their feet as she finished her rendition of "Se Acaso Você Chegasse" and the meal was on the house.

We left the restaurant and walked through the dark streets. The night was warm and balmy. The wine we had drunk relaxed us and there was genuine warmth from Elsie as she held my arm tightly, singing quietly as the cool breeze moved her hair gently away from her face.

"Harry" she said, looking up into my eyes, her lips slightly parted. "I have a friend who lives very nearby. She works in the evening but should be there to let us in. Could we go to her house now? We'll have to rush. I don't think I can wait."

"Not a problem." Thinks I. In fact I thought the whole business was way overdue.

We set off at a slightly faster pace and within a minute had arrived at a small wood-panelled house a few feet from the road with a tiny front garden holding a few small shrubs. The light was on and Elsie knocked loudly on the door which was quickly opened to let us in to a pleasant sitting room. Elsie pushed past the occupier, a tall dark-skinned woman, clearly of African extraction and rushed into the toilet leaving me with the householder.

From the smallest room Elsie called out "Alisha. This is my friend Harry."

I looked at my new acquaintance. Her eyes had an upward oriental slant giving her round face a mysterious and intimidating look. Or perhaps that was because she stood over six foot tall in her stockinged feet and was built like an Olympic athlete. A big-breasted Olympic athlete, I mean.

She was just about to leave for work, I presumed, as she put on the largest pair of high-heels I had ever seen outside those worn by a particularly large Pantomime Dame one year in Brighton. She seemed to have taken to me straight away. It happened that she didn't come across many men who could look her in the eye. Most of them only came up to her chest, she explained later, and looking at her chest I could see that many would find that to be a perfectly satisfactory experience.

Just then there was another knock on the door. This time it was the back door. A cold chill ran down my spine. Call it prescience of you know what that means. If you don't I'll tell you. It means that what had been looking like a dead cert with Elsie was now looking as if it wasn't going to happen and sure enough, limping through the rear entrance, came Manuel. All smiles as he greeted me and asked where Elsie was.

Alisha explained with a rich laugh. "She's in the toilet. She was so desperate she nearly knocked me over to get in there."

So that was it. I had been betrayed. Elsie was in a rush to get to her friend's house not because she was overcome with desire for a piece of Harry but because she'd been caught short. The plan all along was to use me as a decoy whilst Manuel made his way to Alisha's house for a bit of extra-marital nookie. How could he be so two-faced? What had I ever done to him (other than trying to seduce his girl-friend, of course)? In his hand was Elsie's note from the restaurant. Infamy!

"Come on" said Alisha. "You may as well come with me."

"Aren't you off to work?" I asked. I didn't fancy spending all night watching her make card-board boxes in some factory sweat-shop but then she didn't look dressed for a night on the factory floor. More likely she was dressed for a night on the dance-floor.

As soon as Elsie was out of the bathroom the two lovers set about a game of limpet lips and with a casual wave they bade us farewell. Alisha led me into the street and we got into her small car. There was hardly room for the pair of us, both big people, to get in. I leaned my head to the side to fit under the roof while Alisha's hair was flattened to look like a black beret. The front seats were pushed as far back as they could go leaving no leg-room at the back. I looked over at the back seats and remarked with a chuckle "There isn't much room on that back seat." With a cheeky smile and a knowing look she replied "Enough."

Alisha was good company and laughed at almost everything on the journey to work; including a dog that had been run over and lay dead by the road-side. She constantly wore a big grin with her pearly-white teeth glowing in the moonlight. It was infectious and I found the journey most enjoyable despite that the tiny car weaved along the road as she barely bothered to look ahead. I suggested that she should keep her eyes on the road. She answered "Why? It hasn't changed since last night. Anyway. There are better things to look at." She squeezed my upper thigh.

Eventually we arrived at her place of work. She knocked on a solid wooden door and a tiny, inset flap was quickly opened and shut. Her identity checked the door was opened and a suited individual with a nasty jagged scar across his right cheek allowed us through. He looked at me with distaste.

"Americano?" he asked.

"Inglesi" Alisha replied and a smile burst onto the doorman's face.

"Inglesi, welcome. Football ees good, yes?"

"Yes." I replied cautiously "Football."

That seemed to satisfy him and he moved forward to hug me. I am sure there was a gun in his pocket. His jacket pocket. I was glad I wasn't Americano. I mean American.

It took a while for me to adjust to the dim light in the casino, for that was what it was. Alisha set to working at the blackjack table. Dealing the cards and collecting the punter's cash with deft hands. The scantily clad waitresses served drinks to the middle-aged tourists who leered openly at them. I ordered a drink and tried a line on one of the girls but she just looked at Alisha who shook her head, slowly, as a warning and the girl moved away. I had a turn or two at the roulette but with no luck. When I tried the blackjack Alisha sent me away. She said that I couldn't gamble at her table in case I won. The management wouldn't like that. Thinking about the fellow with the gun I felt it better not to take a chance. The evening looked as if it was going to be a bit slow so I settled into a corner to have a drink and enjoy the view. It was a fine view but my thoughts turned to Elsie and Manuel back at Alisha's place. That lucky devil was having a great time while I was stuck here drinking and admiring beautiful girls. The world was not a fair place. Just as I began to feel sorry for myself things took a turn for the worse. Suddenly there was shouting coming from the main entrance. I had never heard a gun fired before so as soon as the first shot was fired I fair near soiled myself. I dropped to the floor beneath the table, stopped breathing and listened intently. There were no more gunshots and a moment later Alisha was standing next to where I lay.

"It's Ok. It's the Police." She told me. "It's a raid. It happens now and then. Stand up."

I stood up to see that about thirty armed police had taken strategic positions around the room. The doorman was being held by his arms by two aggressive looking officers. He was not resisting. The lights were on full and the punters, mainly tourists, stood fearful in the middle of the room. A press photographer took photographs at random. The chief police officer addressed them in fairly good English.

"You are all under arrest for gambling. Which is illegal here and punishable by up to five years in prison. You will all be taken to the police station. First you will come into this office (he indicated a small room at the back of the building) to be interviewed. One by one the tourists were led fearfully into the room. The police did not seem interested in the locals. After around five minutes each tourist came out of the room and was led silently out of the front door by a police officer. I was the last foreigner taken into the office and was very pleased that Alisha was allowed to come with me. The police captain sat behind a small desk. At his right was a large policemen standing loosely to attention with his gun most prominent.

"Americano?" asked the captain.

"Inglesi" I replied – I was picking up the lingo you notice!

At this point Alisha interrupted and seemed to be explaining to the Captain that I wasn't so much a punter more a guest of hers. In fact she demonstrated how close we were with a number of hugs, putting her arm around my waist and drawing me towards her with affection. The Captain seemed to waver but was not completely convinced. It seems I would have to pay a fine. At this point Alisha leaned towards the Captain and, drawing him towards her with a conspiratory move of her fingers, began whispering in his ear. I caught the words "Amigo" which means friend and "Garrincha" which must have been good because that seemed to impress the Captain but not much else made sense. As Alisha returned to my side the Captain leant back in his chair and gave me a thoughtful look. After a few seconds he said he had made his decision and that he would award clemency. I must pay a fine, though. Did I have American dollars? He asked. As it happened I did have about ten so I moved my hand to my jacket pocket to take out my wallet. In a flash the big policemen had drawn his gun and pointed it at me. I am sorry to have to tell you that with the shock of seeing a gun pointing at me my bowels opened temporarily and a ripping fart reverberated across the room. Now with all the spicy food and beer I'd been drinking my movements had become pretty potent and as a result of the fumes which had exploded from my nether regions the gun-toting copper was temporarily incapacitated by a fit of coughing. Alisha let go of my arm and retreated, coughing to a corner of the room while the Captain, clearly a man of greater control, put his hand up to cover his mouth and nose and after a moment cried out "Alright, Inglesi, we surrender! Don't do that again for God's sake."

I suppose I could have grabbed the gun and made a desperate attempt to shoot my way out but firstly I am a footballer not James Bond and secondly the tension in the room had completely disappeared as the other three were all gasping for fresh air and laughing, then gasping again. Eventually the Captain regained his composure long enough to say. "Ok. Pay a ten dollar fine and get out of here, you two."

I looked in my wallet. "Actually I've only got seven" I explained.

"OK. OK. Just pay seven and get out of here before you go off again."

As we left the Captain scooped up the seven dollars and placed them into a small sack which appeared to be full of banknotes. Clearly the other tourists hadn't been so lucky with the size of their fines. But that's South American justice for you. Alisha explained that those who could afford to pay the on-the-spot fine were released. Those who couldn't or wouldn't pay would find themselves in front of a judge in the morning and he would take a lot more to bribe than the local police. Their arrest would also satisfy the locals that something was being done about the illegal activities in the city. In between raids the police kept away from the casino so everybody who mattered was happy and it kept the taxes down. Even the tourists went home with a story to tell. So what's the problem?

The Casino was closed for the night so Alisha and I left for a local bar. She decide to give Elsie and Manuel some more time together and I didn't mind spending more time in her company. She wasn't shy and by the time we'd finished the first bottle of wine we'd become very friendly and I allowed her hand to creep up my thigh to take an estimate of what was on offer. I assure you she was not disappointed. In fact she was so keen to sample the goods that we left the bar soon afterwards but, when we returned to her home, the lights were on but dimmed.

"They are still in there." She said. "We'll have to find something to do for the next hour or so. I have an idea." She re-started the engine and drove a short way to a quiet piece of waste land.

"What are you doing?" I asked as she leaned over and pulled the buttons on my shirt open.

"What do you think?" a muffled voice came from my stomach area.

"But not in this car. There's not enough room."

"Yes there is" she replied, nipping me playfully. And she was right.

Professional sportsmen, real sports I mean not Snooker and Darts, are used to taking knocks. Even running can be a bit physical with elbows flying to gain an advantage and it hasn't been beyond a swimmer to grab somebody's leg to give themselves an advantage. That's why these athletes sometimes have to run and swim in lanes – it stops them from fighting, I'm told. Well I've taken some punishment in my time but that night with Alisha in the car was the worst beating I had taken in my whole life. In order to complete the act it was necessary to open all the windows and to put some feet outside. I lost the skin of the inside of both my ankles, the handbrake had punctured the small of my back and I had a bruise on my forehead the size of an apple where I had been thrown onto the gearstick in a moment of her passion. I can't remember how I lost a handful of hair from the back of my head but I'm guessing it had something to do with the grip she held on me throughout. But to her credit she made me some lovely eggs in the morning.

I returned to my hotel later that day to find that Elsie had checked out. Reception passed me a hand-written note. I have it here:

> Dear Harry
>
> It is time for me to move on. Thank you for all you have done for us.
>
> Another time, another place and maybe you and I .... but you are such an honourable English gentlemen. The thought would never have entered your noble head.
>
> With Love
>
> Elza x x x

How could she have misjudged me? But then maybe she was right. Noble Harry Barker! A gentleman among gentlemen..... but amongst the ladies I'm not so sure.

I re-joined the England team at their hotel the following morning. The lads looked pretty sharp so I guessed they had been laying off the booze while I had been gone. I was exhausted but as soon as I walked through the door I could sense something was wrong. Some of the younger lads were having a bit of a chuckle whilst the older ones looked disapprovingly at me. Almost as if they knew where I'd been and what I'd been up to. But how could they?

Bobby called out to me. "Walter wants a word with you!"

Walter? The England manager? What could he want with me? Now I'll admit it to you, but don't repeat it, for a short moment I wondered if one of the key players had been injured and maybe, just maybe, being thousands of miles from home and being the only English professional footballer available Walter had decided to call me up to the squad. Come on – you've all had that same dream haven't you? You're just walking into the stadium and a head pops out of the window and says "Oi, You! Come in and get changed. You're playing!" But then, being realistic, it was more likely that Walter would put his own boots on and play than give me a game.

I set off to find Walter. I was curious to hear what he had to say.

I found him with two Football Association Officials. Pemberton was one of those typical administrators from within the F.A. Short, plump, middle aged, dark-rimmed glasses, balding with hair that formed a sun-shelter for each ear but left nothing on top to protect his crown. This, all topped off, with wringing hands and a worried frown which over the years had carved ridges into his forehead deepening no doubt every time a new postage stamp had been bought from a budget or a shirt creased. The other official, Passmore, reminded me of a busy squirrel cautiously nibbling at a nut as he looked nervously around. He matched Pemberton for height but topped him for hair, having a full head of trimmed and oiled black hair. He looked as if the heaviest thing he had lifted in a fortnight would have been a comb. The game's in good hands there, I thought.

"There you are, you bloody idiot!" bellows Walter "What have you been up to?"

I wasn't getting a game, then.

"Nothing." I lied with ease. "I've been doing some scouting. Looking for talent." Not entirely untrue that. It depends what you mean by scouting and talent.

"Oh, really!" he replied. "Then what's this?" and with that he threw down a pile of newspapers. On the front page of the first one there was a photograph of me landing at Viña Del Mar airport with Elsie on my arm. She looked good and I looked pretty pleased about it.

I turned to the second newspaper. Again on the front page there was a photograph of Elsie and me. This time we were out shopping. The headline seemed to say something about "Elsa's New Love." I think they meant me!

They showed me the next day's paper. It was much the same with a photograph of Elsie and me at the beach, but it was only on Page 5 which was a disappointment. We had obviously lost some of our star appeal. Pemberton took a moment to admire her figure. He looked up at me with, I must say, a glint of admiration. I thought he isn't as daft as he looks but I found out later I was wrong. Passmore, however, stood away looking disdainfully at the newspapers, his nose raised as if there was a bad smell somewhere in the room. It could have been me, I suppose. I was still having some trouble down below.

Then the tone of the newspapers changed. There was a photograph of me with Elsie but next to it another snap of me with Alisha in the casino. I think the headline read something like "Elsa's love Rat." Me again, I'm afraid.

And then the next paper had the same photograph of Elsie, but this time they had caught her at a bad moment because she looked unhappy whilst next to it was a photograph of me with Blondie and her pal. It seemed that my reputation as a gentleman was under attack.

"I can explain" I began. But I couldn't. "Well, what's the problem?" I asked. "I mean, alright, I wasn't out looking for football players but what has this got to do with the team?"

"I'll explain." Says Walter. "This Elsa that you've been knocking around with was thought by everybody to be the girlfriend of a fellow called Manuel Dos Santos. Commonly known as Garrincha. Which, if you are interested, means 'little bird'."

I was. I finally realised what Manuel had found funny. I couldn't resist a little chuckle but Walter cut me short.

"Garrincha is one of the best footballers on the planet. He is the fellow that taught Pele how to play international football. Now until you stepped into the fray the Brazilian Football Federation were under a lot of pressure to send this Garrincha fellow home in disgrace. He is a married man and the Brazilian people don't like their football stars to be openly unfaithful to their wives. Especially wives with five children!

Blimey, I thought, that lad puts in a full day!

"But as you have been seen running round with this Elsa it has put him in the clear and he is all set to play in the World Cup. I hope, for your sake, he doesn't have a good tournament." He looked angrily at me and I thought it best to make an exit.

"I don't think he will." I replied. "I doubt he'll have the energy."

I left as a glass ash-tray disintegrated on the wall just where I had been standing.

England played Brazil in the quarter finals. Pele was injured on the day and England were highly fancied to go on to win the cup. Garrincha played one of the best games of his life, scoring two and setting up another as Brazil beat England 3-1 and went on to become World Champions.

Well done, little fellow. I bet I know how you and Elsa celebrated.

Everything has a Price

As it is relevant to what happened later in my story I should tell you a little tale about another incident that happened whilst I was in Chile. The first game in England's campaign was against Hungary in the town of Rancagua. The England squad had moved there whilst I was enjoying what the coast had to offer.

Pemberton was full of surprises. Six thousand miles from home this little man was missing his wife and family so much that he felt the need to seek companionship elsewhere. For some reason, as he explained in a private moment, he had decided that I was just the fellow to introduce him to the locals. Now normally Pemberton wasn't the sort of fellow that I would want to spend time with but everybody else was pre-occupied with the football tournament and that left me pretty much out of things. Some of the journalists were keen to buy me a drink to see if I would spill some of the player's secrets but I'd rather buy my own drink than take favours from those people. Even I have got limits. So when Pemberton offered to pay for the taxis and to pick up the bar tabs I took it as the best offer I would get and off we went. Me, Pemberton and his expense account. That'll do nicely.

Pemberton couldn't take his drink and so after a couple of hours in one of the better nightclubs I left him in the arms of a rather worn, but well-dressed, prostitute. He seemed happy that he'd pulled and I wasn't going to disillusion the fellow by explaining that she was only after his money. Come to think of it what woman isn't primarily interested in the size of a fellow's wad?

The nightclub had a resident photographer and I decided that Pemberton was having such a great time that he'd want a memento. The snaps would be delivered to me at the hotel the following morning. The photographer took some great shots, especially the one where Pemberton tripped and fell face first into the woman's deep cleavage. She helped him upright and while he straightened his glasses she slipped her hand into his jacket pocket and removed his wallet. Silly man. Lucky for him that good old Harry Barker was there to take care of him.

I strolled over and took her by the hand that held the wallet. She wasn't that bad looking so I whispered a proposal in her ear. Pemberton had nearly passed out. We took him to his table and placed enough cash inside his jacket pocket to cover his taxi fare back to the hotel. With him comfortable for the night I set off with my new companion and the intent to give her the opportunity to earn the contents of Pemberton's wallet honestly and how God had intended. And so she did. It was worth every penny if you ask me.

I woke in my own hotel room the next afternoon. Pemberton was knocking at my door and calling out for me. He looked awful. Apparently he had just returned to the hotel having had to walk back from the nightclub. It seems some heartless bastard had taken the little money that we'd left him and he had been four hours walking through the blistering heat of a Chilean summer morning. Outrageous! You can't trust anybody, can you?

He explained "It was that woman I was with." He was whispering a bit too loudly so I invited him onto my room.

"Yes." I owned "I remember her. You seemed to be getting along really well together."

"Well." He sobbed "That cow stole my wallet. It had my money and all my personal documents. It even has a photograph of my wife. What'll I do?"

I'd seen the photograph and, frankly, I thought he was better off without it. It reminded me of a picture I once saw of Chuck Wepner after he had gone fifteen rounds with Muhammad Ali. And, yes, I know Wepner had a moustache.

"Now listen" says I "why don't we report this to the police?"

I could have told him the answer to that, but, no need. Pemberton of the Football Association was sufficiently on-the-ball.

"If I report this to the police then word would get back to those other bastards, I mean my fellow FA officials, and then, God forbid, one of them gits is bound to grass to my wife." Clearly the FA was an establishment run by men of the highest calibre holding mutual respect for their fellows but, like I say, I'd seen the photo of his wife and I wouldn't fancy Pemberton's chances in any contest other than a sprint.

"Let's go back to the night-club and ask around." I suggested "Somebody there is bound to know something about her."

"Do you think so?" Pemberton asked, his puppy-like eyes watered as they looked up into mine, his balding head glistened with perspiration. "Yes." He mused "Somebody there may know something." He was desperately grasping for a way out while I resisted the desire to chuckle. There was indeed somebody who knew something, of course. I did. I knew where she lived, which way it was from her bedroom to the lav and quite a bit about the contents of her underwear when she was wearing it. I also knew that Pemberton's wallet was safely tucked away, minus expenses of course, in my bed-side cabinet. But there was no need to spoil things by letting Pemberton off the hook quite yet.

Well, I dressed and made my way casually down to reception where Pemberton and I had agreed to meet. As I arrived and glanced around the mosaic floored hallway I heard a whisper emanating from behind a mock-roman pillar. A bony finger attempted to distract me from the tall, dark-haired white-bloused receptionist (how good they look with the white-laced bras clearly visible through the thin cloth. But I digress.)

It was Pemberton. Predictably he had no intention of re-visiting the night club. He had a thousand excuses. Somebody may see him in daylight. He was needed for an important meeting. He was expecting an important phone call. He had a whitlow on his finger. In short he wanted dear old Harry, his best pal, the only man he could trust, the one true person in the whole of football, no, in the whole of Britain, no, in the whole wide world. He wanted this knight in shining armour, this Galahad, this saintly man to pop off down to the local knocking shop, track down a thieving whore and retrieve a philandering drunk's wallet. Fair enough, thinks I, I'm just the man for the job.

Once I'd agreed and Pemberton had promised undying gratitude and favours and, most importantly, to cover all of my incidental expenses I set off in a taxi. I couldn't resist instructing the taxi driver of my destination loudly enough for all in Reception to hear. I enjoyed seeing Pemberton cringe and disappear up the stairs two at a time.

Of course I changed my destination as soon as the taxi driver set off. I had an hour or so to kill to make it look good. Now what could I do to pass the time. The answer was obvious and I'm sure you've guessed - straight round to her place for another tumble. Once again, expenses charged to Pemberton. He'll owe me a pretty penny by the time we get back to dear old Blighty.

Back Home – again

On my return I took the wallet out of my drawer and slipped it into Pemberton's sweaty palm. I explained that I'd had to pay the girl a hefty price to get it back and she'd cleaned out all the cash. It was the best I could do and he was mightily grateful, although quite shocked at the debt he had run up with me. I noted a suspicious look in his eyes but it didn't bother me. I already had the photographs, you see, so there'd be no double-dealing by this particular pillar of society. I had him by the short-and-curlies alright. Talking about short-and-curlies it transpired that mine had come into contact with some unwelcome visitors. That'll teach me to be a bit more careful who I share recreational facilities with. A quick visit to the local quack sorted it out though and I promised myself to be more selective in future. And I was, until the next time.

It was a long miserable journey back home. We made the best of it by drinking ourselves into a stupor. Well I did anyway. The thing about long journeys is that as you gaze out of the window, whether it be a train, car or plane, and see the world go by it becomes too easy to start thinking about the world and your place in it and the future. You may think about the people that you've done down and regret it. You may also think about the people that have done you down – and regret that even more. I even found myself thinking about Rose and Stan Shadwell. Married and doing nicely. Then Doreen Brennan, and her maniacal father. I shuddered and opened another bottle. Them bastards at Bradford. Mum and all my uncles. I opened another bottle. I needed to make something of my life. I'd never make it as a top footballer. I looked around at Charlton, Greavsie and the rest. They're actually good at this and what's more they seem to care. I just did this because it was a way to pick up the birds and because it beat working my fingers to the bone in a factory. I shuddered and opened another bottle. My eyes rested on Pemberton and the big-nobs at the front and that was when it hit me. Or was it Greavsie hit me and accused me of nicking one of his beers. It was time to go back home and visit Mum.

Everybody says it – the place looks smaller when you return home. Well my bedroom looked smaller all-right. Mum had taken half of it away and had it converted into an inside lavatory with a high-level cistern placed just the other side of the flimsy plasterboard wall that separated my bed from the toilet. My feet hung over the end of my tiny single bed. How had I ever slept in this house with the constant noise of people either making their way excitedly towards the pub at the end of the street or making their way even more noisily back a few hours later?

I took the time to visit some of my old haunts and ended up in Barnston Snooker Hall. From the door at the top of the stairs it looked much the same, maybe just a bit dingier, if that was possible, and they appeared to have re-spotted the stairway with fresh blood. I had a few games. I'd improved. I managed to beat one of the locals twice before he offered to play me for a small wager in order to give the game and edge. I explained that I just needed to pop into the toilets to check in a mirror in case the word "mug" was written on my forehead. He didn't appreciate the joke and seemed to feel aggrieved that he'd wasted an hour setting me up for a sting only to be thwarted. Steer clear of trouble today, I thought and I offered to buy him a drink by way of making peace. He accepted my offer but possibly only because a couple of teenage lads had made their way into the hall, having taken an unofficial leave of absence from school no doubt, clutching their glistening new snooker cues. He honed in on them like a sparrow-hawk to a fledgling.

I ordered a couple of pints, deciding to watch the fellow fleece the young lads. It was a quiet day and I was in no rush to get back to Mum's house. I stood at the bar hardly noticing the poorly dressed figure crouched over his near finished pint at the bar. The hustler took his drink from me with a wink and returned to watch the boys playing. He complimented them regularly, building rapport. He placed a coin on the side of the table – a challenge. Winner stays on. The boys concentrated harder. Both wanting to be the one to pick up the gauntlet, as well as not losing face in front of this pleasant stranger who somehow had managed to identify their real talent as future champions. I sipped my insipid ale and noticed the quiet man still nestling the dregs of his pint. Looking straight ahead, his eyes seemingly fixed on the optics at the back of the bar.

"You don't know who I am. Do you?"

I was tempted to say "No" and leave it at that but I thought I'd better be polite and added "Should I?"

"You should." He answered and continued to try to bore a hole into the optics with his eyes.

"There's a lot of things I should do" says I "and a lot of things I shouldn't." (Who says the common man has no wit?)

A long pause. He's dropped off to sleep, I thought, and signalled the bar man for a re-fill.

"That's right. Get yourself a drink." My new companion granted his permission.

I couldn't fault his observation skills. He was right in saying I was right. We were both right. I <u>was</u> getting myself a drink.

He raised his own glass and replaced it onto the bar. He had hardly wet his lips. He seemed determined to make that last drop in the bottom of the glass see him through to closing time.

Never let it be said that I couldn't take a hint. "Alright" I says, making one of the biggest mistakes of my life. "You tell me who you are and I'll fill up your glass."

"You fill up my glass" says he "and I'll tell you who I am and who you are."

"How about I half fill your glass then because I already know who I am?" The humour was wasted on him and he didn't say another word until the barman had poured him a pint of mild. I would have offered to buy him something a bit more palatable but had the impression that if I got him used to up-market brews like a Watney's Red Barrel he'd never be able to go back to the rough stuff. He should stick with what he was used to.

His name was Brian Freeman. He was an ex-pro who had spent his career in the lower leagues, retiring in his early thirties with legs that could hardly see him walk to the bus stop. He knew me from my time in Manchester. I think he'd been at the meeting when I told Jimmy the Chin to sort out the minimum wage business. I've told you about that, haven't I? Anyway he went on and on about how football had done him down and how he had nothing and how it had left him crippled with no way of earning a living.

I stopped listening for a while noticing that one of the truants had beaten the hustler for a second time. The play was on. The hustler complained that there was no edge to the game. He suggested a shilling to make it interesting. It ended up being half a crown. The non-playing schoolboy came to the bar and ordered a pint. The barman, unmoved, asked him if he had a letter from his mum saying he could drink. Confused as to whether the answer to that was "Yes" or "No" the lad beat a retreat, returning to the table where the hustler was having terrible luck. It seemed he kept missing his shots and leaving the ball just over the pocket for John Pulman's next challenger to convert.

I returned to my pint and the one-sided conversation to hear a few words which struck home. "Of course," said my companion "if I had a stake I could make a fortune. I know People you see!"

"What do you mean?" I inquired and he signalled that another drink was required before he would say more. "Why not?" I thought. "I've got all day."

It turned out that Brian did know people, lots of people, in the game. He knew who was straight and who could be bought. He knew a few players that felt, like him, that they had to get what they could out of the game whilst they could. It all came down to betting. Not through the bookies. Back-street betting. There was a fellow around who had made a lot of money from punters by taking bets on football matches. Most of the pubs and clubs around had somebody who was prepared to take a bet but the word was that one fellow was behind all the gambling in that part of Yorkshire. If only I'd known who it was I wouldn't have touched his idea with a bargepole. But I was young and had done well out of a bit of iffy gambling before. This didn't sound too risky.

The hustler had lost his half-crown to the schoolboy. "Play again?" asked the hustler. "Double or quits." The balls were racked up, the cues chalked and the hook was in the snapper's mouth. I wondered if the lad would be leaving with his trousers.

"See that lad". I nodded towards the schoolboy. Brian didn't turn his gaze from the optics. "He's going to lose every penny he has got."

"He's a chump" replied Brian "but you're not. I know who you are and how you work. I've been watching you and, like I said, I know people. If you come in with me you'll never put in more than you take out. You can handle all the money and give me a share."

I thought about it. I finished my pint.

"There's no rush" he said. "The season don't start for a few weeks. You think on and let me know. You'll find me here most days." Oddly he had about as much left in his glass as he had when I had first seen him. His eyes moved from the optics to the dregs.

I made my way to the door just as the hustler doubled the black the length of the table to win the game. "That was lucky!" he exclaimed "At last I've won one. I'd better quit now. You're too good for me."

"Hang on" cried his young mark. "Give me a chance to get my money back."

I caught the hustler's eyes as I reached the stairs. They glistened.

Prosperity

What does it mean to be a "Professional"?

Somebody told me once that it meant doing what had to be done to get the job done. Somebody else said it meant being paid for what you were doing. Brian seemed to have some ideas about "professionalism". He'd had his fill as an honest player being paid a pittance while cash was being stuffed into brown envelopes and safes all over the country. There were back-handers happening everywhere in football but the players saw so little of it. Managers were creaming a little off the top of transfer deals. Famous names were taking tax-free incentives and there were some referees, it was said, who could be bought.

Fixing a football match isn't as easy as you might think. There are eleven players on both sides. No one player can be relied on to both score a goal and to let one in. If a defender or goalie contrives to let the ball slip between his legs then there's always the risk that some chump playing up front will decide to have a good day and score a hat-trick. Linesmen, or should I say Assistant Referees, can rule players on and off side at will but they can't put the ball at the players feet nor make sure he scores with it. There is only so much that can be done. Let's take a minute to look at the position of the Referee from the point of view of a policeman. MMO it is called. Means, motive and opportunity. Does a referee have the means to sway a game? Sure he does and it doesn't have to be as obvious as a poor penalty decision or a sending off. Let one side tackle as forcefully as they like whilst as soon as the other team puts in a strong challenge it's a yellow card. Give an equal number of free kicks – but for one side it's only in safe areas whilst for the other it always gives an opportunity to score a goal. If things go badly wrong then a referee can always resort to a red card or a soft penalty, there are always opportunities in a football match. Every time a corner is taken there is so much pushing and shoving in the penalty area that the referee can take his pick either to give a free-kick to the defending side or a penalty to the attackers.

But what motive might a referee have to sway a result? In the normal course of events not a lot. Managers and players try to influence them from the moment they are given the fixture. You know the kind of thing. "Just a quiet word before the game, Ref. Watch their Number 4 – he is always tugging at a shirt and taking an ankle." Or "You know about their Number 9 don't you, Ref? He squeals like a pig every time somebody goes near him. You won't let him con you, will you Ref?" It can be more subtle than that, too. A "Well done, Ref" every time a decision is given for you and then no words but a disappointed look and a tiny shake of the head when a decision goes to the opposition. The Refs know all this of course but they are only human. Today a top professional referee can earn around £100,000 a year. It sounds a lot but some of the players on the park (youngsters, mind you) will be earning more than that between a Sunday and a Friday, regardless of whether or not there's a mid-week game. Then, when they do play, these kids, still with traces of milk from their Mother's teet on their faces, feel they have the right to abuse the referee every time a decision goes against them.

Put yourself in the position of a referee – if somebody offered you a five-figure sum in a numbered Swiss account for the sake of a few careful decisions you'd have to think about it, wouldn't you? I know I would and I can't be the only one. But that's these days. When I played football the referees were on a pittance and no doubt could have used a few extra quid but the problem wasn't the money. It was finding the right referee. You didn't want a referee going to the authorities after a game saying that somebody had offered him cash for favours. Nor, come to think of it, do you want a team of honest professionals, like Wolves in the seventies, being insulted by the offer of a brown envelope and then going out and playing like demons to make sure the crooks didn't succeed.

It was all a bit risky this corruption lark so, my curiosity aroused, I turned up at the snooker hall the next afternoon to hear what Brian had to say. He was the only person there and was leaning on the bar at the same spot nestling, possibly, the same dregs. I bought him another pint. He raised his finger to his lips to indicate silence whilst the barman was within earshot. When the barman returned to the cellars to resume his work of restocking Brian led me into the toilets. He checked both cubicles to make sure we could not be overheard. He looked outside the door twice just in case somebody had entered the hall.

"This conversation never took place." He informed me.

"What conversation?" I asked.

"This one" He checked the cubicles again.

"Right." I said.

"You don't repeat this to anyone, OK?"

"OK" I replied.

"We've never met."

I began to wish we hadn't. "Right." Says I. "Shall I make a note of that?"

He nearly had an apoplexy "DON'T WRITE ANYTHING DOWN" he whispered in capitals through gritted teeth.

"This is what we'll do" at last he was getting to the point. He checked outside the door again. "The next time you are going to play for Leeds, you get in touch with me."

"Right" says I again. He turned from me and opened the toilet door as if to leave. "Hang on. Is that it?"

He slammed the door shut and grabbed my shoulders "Fer Christ's sake! Keep it down! Somebody could have heard you! We've got to keep this quiet. Even the walls have ears!"

I looked and he was right. Somebody had drawn a pornographic picture of Mickey and Minnie Mouse on the toilet wall. Ten out of ten for art work but I am not sure that the snooker playing public were the right audience for this version of Steamboat Willie.

Brian opened the door and checked left and right before he slipped out of the toilet. If anybody had seen him doing that they'd have made an assumption about what we were doing in the lav which would be a lot worse for us both than simply making arrangements to meet at a later date. Old Etonians were being locked up for similar misdemeanours in London lavatories all the time. Not something that would do my reputation a lot of good.

I'd heard enough from Brian. I left quietly without saying goodbye partly to give Brian the impression that I was keen to keep our subterfuge a secret and partly because I had concluded that he was suffering from the effects of too many headed clearances. I thought little more about the whole business until one Monday afternoon a few weeks into the season when I caught sight of him loitering outside our training ground.

As expected I'd started in the Reserves, again, but a terrible run of injuries in the squad during pre-season games and those picked up in the first game of the season (where the lads had done marvellously well to beat much fancied Stoke, away) had brought me to the fore. It was almost certain that I would be given a rare start in our first home game of the season against Rotherham on the Wednesday evening. Hopes were high and there was a buzz around the place as the belief that we could get promotion back up into Division 1 grew. I know I haven't mentioned Leeds' relegation the previous season. It's not something footballers like to hark on about so I'll move on. The Rotherham game was going to be part of a double-header. This week we would meet Rotherham at home and next Tuesday we would travel the 30 miles south to return the favour. On the Saturday in between we were going to entertain Sunderland.

There is always a lot of pressure and a full house for the first game of a season. Everybody is hopeful of a good start and a stab at promotion, or in Rotherham's case, a good start to provide a cushion against relegation. The colourful fans turn out with their scarves and rattles cheering and jeering. They stop for a pint or two on the way. Dads lift young lads on their shoulders and the sun beats down brightly, evaporating the urine spilled on the street corners as thousands of Yorkshire-folk stagger drunkenly towards the ground. A great day out for the whole family.

Now I can honestly tell you that I had no intention of engaging with Brian on this or any other crazy venture. Not, of course, because fixing football matches was morally reprehensible, illegal and probably doomed to failure but because the man was clearly tuppence short of a shilling and because I was scared of getting caught. A quick word of advice, now, for anybody out there currently considering doing something which is reprehensible and illegal. If you are going to partner up with someone make sure they have got a full set of marbles and can be trusted. Thinking about it though – if you and your pal are about to do something dishonest then let's face it, at least one of you can't be trusted. Think on!

In the case of the Rotherham game the reality was that neither of Brian or I could be trusted. He caught up with me at the bus stop. A couple of the lads were with me so he said nothing. He got on the bus but while me and the lads clambered upstairs so they could smoke he sat on the lower floor guarding the entrance. Shortly after I alighted he came up behind me.

"Hang on." He said "What's the rush? We've got some business to do."

I turned to face him. "Look." I said "I know we had a bit of a chat the other week but it was just a bit of a laugh for me. I'm not sure what you're up to but I'm not really interested. I'm going to be playing on

Wednesday night and I need to focus on my game." (Always the professional, you see.) "So, you know, thanks for the offer. You're welcome to the pint I bought you – I'll see you around."

I thought that was pretty clear but he didn't seem to take the hint. He followed me and tugged at my sleeve.

"It's not as simple as that." He was now blocking my path. "A deal's been done. You're committed."

"You ought to be committed!" I replied. (I still had it. The quick repartee. I should have been on the stage. In fact, come to think of it if I'd known how sticky things were going to get I'd have got on any stage out of town.) "I'm not doing anything daft for you or anybody else."

"Oh no?" his eyes narrowed in the manner of a man who knew something that I didn't. That was because he did know something that I didn't. "You'll do as you are told. Mr A. has got money riding on the result of Wednesday's game and he expects you to make sure his money isn't wasted."

Mention of Mr A.'s name gave me a bit of a start. My stomach tightened. I thought of his "operatives" and our meeting in the snooker hall. They were hard men. Not to mention Lurch, the driver.

"Mr A. said that if there was any problem he would send a car for you. Do you know his driver? Used to fight professionally – and I don't mean in a ring."

Blast it. He'd mentioned Lurch, the driver. I wonder if he saw the blood drain out of my face. If he did he probably would have mentioned that blood drawing from my face would be exactly what was to come. Well, I thought, there's no point in Lurch making a trip for nothing. The least I could do was to appear to be prepared to play along.

"OK. I'll do what I can." I answered "But even I can make mistakes. If Rotherham win then I don't want anybody blaming it on me." I had clearly got the wrong end of the stick and to make sure I understood Brian punctuated each of his next words with a poke in my chest.

"When Rotherham win it'll be just as well if nobody blames you."

The "when" was appeared to be the key word and for me the penny dropped half way.

"Hang on a minute. Even with me at the back nobody expects Rotherham to get a win. It just won't happen."

"Then you'd better make sure it does happen." The penny completed its journey south. "The odds on Leeds are rubbish after that win at Stoke but Rotherham are three to one and those are odds that Mr A. likes. There'll be a good payout for you when the result comes in and a payback if it doesn't. You got it?"

I had it alright. I nodded and Brian turned quickly and crossed the road to catch the bus back into town. No Kerb-Drill but where's a speeding police-car when you need one?

We had light training on Tuesday afternoon. Don liked his team to be well prepared for every match and had managed to dig up some information about Rotherham. Who their key players were, what foot they kicked with, who came up for corners, what the centre-forwards girl-friend's name was and, by way of winding him up, some suggestions as to which of us may have been there first. I didn't say anything but I may have known her, so to speak, having met her in a club a few months earlier. I decided not to mention it to the centre-forward. He was a big, mean looking bastard and anyway I had enough on my mind.

I noticed as we left the training ground that opposite the bus stop was a smart looking limousine with darkened windows. The driver's window was wound down and there was Lurch. He turned his head and looked straight at me. Smiled and gave the faintest of nods. The car pulled out, causing a mini driver to swerve, and began to cruise away. The mini driver opened his own window and let loose with a tirade of abuse. "If only you knew, mate. " I thought "You'd turn your car around and put your foot down in the opposite direction."

But the point was well made. Mr A. wanted the result the following evening and he knew where to find me.

I've heard of a School for Scandal and most of you know of the School of Hard Knocks but I haven't yet come across a school where you can learn how to throw a game of football. I could hardly go to the PFA and ask for advice and looking around the dressing room before the game started I couldn't see an old, wise head who could give me some pointers. I'd have to make it up as I went along. If things could be kept tight then maybe I could give the ball away late on and a shock one-nil to Rotherham would be on the cards. The footballing gods seemed to be on my side. Rotherham came out like tigers and took the lead after ten minutes. Perfect and it wasn't even my fault. They'd won a corner and I stayed with the man I was supposed to be marking. The ball went to the back post where our left back was supposed to be marking their right winger. Our left back wasn't there and Rotherham player scored with a simple header. I patted the left back on the shoulder and told him not to worry. I like to be supportive of colleagues.

Glorious Leeds then went at Rotherham with a vengeance. I stayed back but was hardly involved as all the pressure came from the white shirts. The Rotherham defence were like rocks. C'mon the lads! I admired a great clearance which put the ball over my head. I chased after it. I was still quick but the Rotherham centre-forward, a traditional big Number 9, was a bit quicker. I had no intention of deliberately letting him have the ball. It would be too obvious so I made sure I arrived ahead of him and controlled the ball with the outside of my left foot and turned gracefully to my left. He would now sweep past my right shoulder and I would appear as a nimble matador bemusing a lumbering bull. At least that was what was supposed to happen. However the cheating git took my right leg away with a sweep of his left foot. I tumbled to the ground, my ankle on fire. It was an obvious foul but the referee had been caught out of position and was chasing back from the Rotherham penalty area. There was no whistle so the brute took the ball away and headed straight for our goal.

Our brave lads tried to catch him but it was no good. Once he was inside our penalty area he slammed the ball past our goalie to make it 2-0 to Rotherham. Surely nobody could blame me for that? I wondered. Sadly a small, unappreciative, section of the crowd did. My ankle was clearly injured so I was taken off the pitch for treatment. There was no way I could play on.

Our trainer, having applied the full extent of his medical knowledge in the form of the ice-cold wet sponge, could do nothing to relieve the pain. As I lay at the pitch-side convinced my work was done there was a huge cheer from the thirty thousand Leeds supporters that had packed the ground. Somehow the ten men had scored and Leeds were back in the game. At this point I noticed the rather large figure standing at the front of the stand obscuring the view of tens of supporters who were stuck in the morass behind him. It was Lurch. He caught my gaze and indicated with his outstretched thumb that I was to get back onto the pitch. No chances were to be taken and I couldn't influence the game from the sidelines. Clearly Mr A. thought Leeds would be worse off with me on the pitch rather than off the pitch. I couldn't fault his judgment.

So, this brave lad rose painfully to his feet and hobbled towards the pitch. The crowd rose as one (or they would have risen but it was almost all standing in those days) to applaud my dedication to the cause. Any doubts as to my fault in the second goal were dissipated. All was forgiven. All Hail the return of the Conquering Hero!

I did have a bit of a problem, though. My ankle had swollen like a new mother's breast and was equally tender. There was no word of apology from the Rotherham centre-forward and I decided that, given the opportunity, I'd pay him back in kind. Of course Leeds were now piling on the pressure again. Could Rotherham hold out until half-time? Would the Millers (as Rotherham are known) be ground down? (I should have written headlines for the tabloids!)

I can tell you the answer to that. No! By half time Leeds had put so much pressure on Rotherham that the lead had been reversed. Leeds were winning 3-2. One had been an own goal and the other, shortly afterwards, a mistake by their goalkeeper. I began to suspect foul-play!

Half-time gave the trainer the opportunity to work on my injury. He duly found some colder water and applied the sponge to my ankle. He also applied a fresher sponge to my groin which didn't help my ankle but it helped to get me onto my feet. One of the other players foolishly complained of a bruised nose so the sponge was removed from my groin and slapped onto his face. Nobody else had any injuries to be treated.

It was "Well done" all round in the half-time dressing room. The boss was happy and told the lads that the second goal wasn't my fault. We should push on and maybe make it five or six. I timidly suggested that I could do with a bit of cover at the back, what with my ankle and everything but the other players were brimming with confidence. A case of don't worry if they manage to get a goal we're going to score half a dozen. Unfortunately they were probably right.

Rotherham must have had a real bollocking from their manager at half time. They came out roaring like lions and for the first 30 seconds looked as if they were going to take the game to Leeds. Coming out like tigers in the first half had nearly worked so, presumably they had decided to stick with the cat theme. That was until Leeds won the ball and hit the crossbar with a shot from 30 yards out. After that it was corner after corner and desperate saves and clearances.

It was purely a matter of time before Leeds would score again. I couldn't make any difference because I was stuck at the back exchanging scowls with the Rotherham centre-forward. The ball simply wasn't coming our way. But at least Rotherham were holding out and there was still a chance. I was getting anxious, though, and with about fifteen minutes to go the ball was cleared from the Rotherham half, over my head for me to chase. I set off at a fair pace, keeping ahead of the Number 9. My ankle was still painful and affecting my speed. He caught me and in the tradition of the game tugged at my sleeve to pull me off balance. I could see our two full-backs closing in on us. He may get to the ball at the same time as me but there was cover. Cleverly he managed to toe the ball forward as I was about to clear it. It rolled forward into our penalty area.

The goalie started to come out then hesitated. The two full-backs changed direction to intercept the ball based on its new trajectory. Having missed a step I had to try to accelerate in order to catch the Number 9. He was slightly ahead of me as we entered the penalty area. Now was my chance. I stretched forward and took his trailing leg at the ankle. He deserved it. I heard him swear as I crunched home. He fell to the ground as if his leg had been cut from underneath him. Which it had. The Leeds supporters groaned as one. The Rotherham supporters cheered in anticipation of the penalty and the referee waved play-on.

Meanwhile the two full-backs had been distracted by my certain foul and in their haste to intercept the Rotherham player they were approaching each other at full speed. They had no time to slow down and collided, full pelt, with each other and the Number 9. The four of us lay in a heap on the ground inside the penalty area.

Our goalkeeper kicked the ball out of play and on came the trainers. Both full-backs had to be removed from the pitch. My ankle was still painful but their Number 9 jumped up and ran over to the referee, called him blind and demanded a penalty. I almost joined him. I wonder, looking back, if the referee was seeking some justice for me for his own earlier mistake. As they say – it wasn't justice I wanted it was mercy!

Rotherham did the decent thing and returned possession to us from the throw-in but with only 8 fit players plus me on the pitch the tide had turned. Rotherham came out and attacked. We were not organised and from the wing a cross came over and Number 9 headed home. The combined voice of the supporters had turned from joy to trepidation. Some got behind the team and others stood in stunned silence. Rotherham attacked again and won a corner. Now Leeds were under pressure. One of the full-backs returned to the pitch but he was not fully fit and missed a tackle to give a free kick away just outside the penalty area. With everybody back in the area it was an opportunity for me to settle the result. There could only be a few minutes left. The corner came over and Number 9 jumped for it. So did I, right onto his back. I put both my arms around his neck and dragged him to the ground. The ball was being hooked desperately around the goal-mouth but still the referee wouldn't give them a penalty. Number 9 stood up and threw a punch at my head. He had completely lost his cool. Perhaps he knew about me and his girlfriend, I thought in a flash as I ducked. His fist went over my head and just at that moment our goalie punched the ball away from goal straight towards his knuckles and from there it flew into the back of the net. The Rotherham players turned to run back and celebrate their winner. The Leeds players surrounded the referee and complained of handball. The referee pointed at me and indicated that he thought the ball had come off the back of my head. I was being credited with an own goal! Outrageous! Thank God that sometimes our match officials get it right.

After the game the other Leeds players showed me a great deal of sympathy. I had been unlucky, they said, it could have happened to anyone. Good lads they were, every one.

There was no training on the Thursday so I found myself once again in the snooker hall. There was no sign of Brian but as I left the hall the black limousine pulled up along-side me. The rear passenger's window rolled down and a brown envelope was pressed into my hand.

"Good job!" said Mr A. and the car accelerated away.

I opened the envelope at home and smiled. "Thank God that was over" I thought. I was wrong.

My ankle injury meant I was not able to play in the home win against Sunderland on the Saturday but due to recurring injuries to other players I was required for the Tuesday return match at Rotherham. I kept my head down over the weekend, spending time in my room at home. I had made a tidy sum from the game against Rotherham but wasn't happy. This all felt a bit too risky. One thing that was nice was the positive reviews that I received in the national papers. I've kept a couple of them to this day as they were probably the best thing that was ever said about my football. The first was from the "News of the World" which had a reputation for providing incisive insight into the sexual habits of anybody they could catch at it and photographs of any Bimbo that was prepared to "reveal all". The 'paper genuinely has a high reputation for its sports coverage and Frank, their journalist, said "Barker shouldn't be blamed for any of the four goals Leeds conceded. Other players should have helped this novice more." I liked that. It put the blame squarely where it belonged. The other newspaper, the Sunday Times, was a little less effusive in its praise but I still thought them very fair. "Rarely have I seen a professional footballer with Barker's ability. His moderate pace and undeveloped strength are his assets. Other skills such as an ability to read a game and pass a ball are, apparently, not valued by Leeds United. Should Barker develop just a fraction of the ability shown by Moore at West Ham he may yet become a half-decent squad player." I am not sure that I understood all that but I am very proud to have been compared to the great Bobby Moore.

I was quite relieved that the business with Brian was behind me and I quite enjoyed a bit of light training on Monday morning but how disappointed was I, when I returned home from training in the afternoon to see Brian waiting outside my house? I'll tell you – flippin' disappointed indeed!

"I've been looking for you." He smiled. "Good job on Wednesday. Mr A. was very pleased."

"Wonderful." Says I. "What do you want?"

"Tomorrow night. The Rotherham game. You're playing aren't you?"

"I'm not sure." I lied. "It's not likely."

"That's not what I've heard and Mr A. has heard the same. He has put a little bet on and he wants an edge."

"I can't do it again." I pleaded "It's too dangerous."

"Dangerous?" Brian caught my arm. "Do you know what is dangerous? I'll tell you what's dangerous. Mr A. is dangerous."

I knew he was right.

"Shall I tell Mr A. that you can't help him? I don't think he'd be very happy to hear it and maybe he'd feel he should come round here with some of his friends to hear it from you for himself."

Brian had made his point but just in case I wasn't fully convinced he added. "And if, from your hospital bed, you decide to tell everybody how you got there then you'll have to tell them all about last Wednesday. So how do you fancy six months inside? Mr A. has friends there, too."

That was what you might call a winning argument. So I agreed but made it clear this would be the last time. Brian smiled and nodded but somehow I wasn't sure of his sincerity. Perhaps I was being too cynical.

As he walked off he added, pointing at his knee caps. "Oh! And you'd better make sure you play. If you don't it might be your last chance for a very, very long time."

I felt sick in my stomach.

It was an hour on the coach to Rotherham. I was even quieter than normal and hardly raised a complaint when one of the players strung a jock-strap over my head. They were "up-for-it" that night and determined to set things right from the week before. I tried to muster some enthusiasm but I was too terrified even to pretend. Don came over to me as we got off the bus.

"Are you OK lad? Don't worry. I know you will do fine. Forget last week." He patted me on the back and smiled.

How could I let such a nice fellow down? I thought seriously about turning on my ankle or making a run for it. Catching a train down South and joining a circus or something. However I then caught sight of something which caused me to head rapidly for the safety of the stadium player's entrance. There, donkey jacket and all, being held back by the line of policemen which had been assigned to protect us from the local hard-men, was no other than ol' man Brennan. He tried to press between the linked arms of the local constabulary but thankfully the thin blue line held. Well done, Officers! Good job! I hurriedly caught up with my team-mates.

This game was completely different from the match of the previous week. Being at home and having just beaten us Rotherham took control of the game. They pressed us early and held onto the ball. After about fifteen minutes of this I began to relax a bit. Rotherham looked as if they might pull it off without any help from me. If only they could put away one of their chances. My old pal, Number 9, was tapping at my ankles at every opportunity. I wished he would concentrate a bit more on the game and less on kicking me. That way maybe he would score and we'd both be a bit happier. I didn't respond so we avoided all out war. At half-time the score was still nil-nil and then, in the changing rooms Don dropped a bomb-shell.

"I can't believe it." he screamed "I've heard from one of the locals that they reckon there was something funny going on in last week's game! Somebody had taken a back-hander! And I reckon I know who it bloody-well was!" He was clearly furious. His cheeks reddened and his eyes bulged making him look like a red-cheeked bug-eyed thing.

There was a chorus of "Who was it, Boss?" from the team. From all except me of course, because I knew who it bloody-well was."

"Wasn't it obvious?" Don asked. "Think about it!"

I must have physically shrunk. Could I make a run for the door? How could I get away from the ground?

The players looked blankly around. One of them looked at me. I was about to own up. Perhaps if I told them all about Mr A. and his threats they'd understand. Then again perhaps they wouldn't. I kept quiet.

"Who was it, Boss? I'll kill the bastard." The goalie looked accusingly at the rest of the team. My bowels tightened.

"The referee, of course" said Don. "That last goal should never have stood and their first was a foul on Harry, here." He placed a caring hand on my shoulder. The rest of the team looked sympathetically at me as my bowel loosened to release a dreadful stench. "Now" said Don moving briskly away from me "I want you to go out there and show this lot who the better team is. Take no prisoners. We owe them."

Encouraged by both Don and my contribution the team rose as one and noisily trooped out into the fresh air of the warm evening. Don placed a hand on my shoulder and with reference to my wind said "Do something about that will you son? You could have taken out half my front line with that." He gave me a smile and a wink and we both got out before we fainted.

Don knew how to motivate a team. We tore into Rotherham and I got caught up in the excitement so much so that when we took the lead I found myself whooping for joy oblivious to the fact that the goal could have cost me six months either in intensive care or in prison. Number 9 seemed to take it badly and he proceeded to kick me even more often than before. I have to say I was getting fed up with it. I didn't want to touch him so I thought I'd have a dig in another way. As I strolled past him I whispered in his ear "How's your Sandra?"

It caught his attention and the next time he passed me he asked. "What do you mean?"

"Sandra, your girlfriend. Me and some of the lads wondered how she was getting along." He looked at me angrily.

"Piss off!" he suggested but I knew he was hooked. "How do you know her?"

"Not just me, mate. She seems to go for footballers. Frank has been there, Charlie and even Billy" I nodded towards the balding fifty year old trainer. "I wouldn't go back there, though. Not now." And I pointed at his dick.

I then saw an opportunity to make a covering run back towards my goal. Number 9 had forgotten all about the game. He started to walk towards me, then, ignoring everything around him he started to run towards me, shouting abuse. The very least of which was questioning my parentage. I have to be honest, here. I may have said a bit too much and possibly didn't entirely cover myself with glory. As he approached me with murderous intent in his eyes I turned and ran. Some unkind observers said screaming like a girl. Now I did mention that whilst I was quick he was a bit quicker but I can tell you that when the chips were down, and I assure you they were very much on the plate and covered with ketchup, he could not catch me. The problem wasn't getting away from him it was where to go. I completed a half-circuit of the pitch before I realised I was trapped. The game had stopped and the whole stadium watched as this maniac sprinted after me. The referee blew his whistle so I headed in that direction, still being chased. One of the Rotherham players tried to stop him but was bundled out of the way. I reached the referee and tried to hide behind him. The referee tried to prevent the Number 9 from hitting me but was pushed aside. I was then grabbed by my throat but at that time, fortunately, half a dozen players from both sides leaped onto him and wrestled him to the ground. I took the opportunity to surreptitiously give him a small kick in the ribs. I owed him at least that. Eventually he was dragged from the pitch. The referee sent him off and Rotherham were now one-nil down with only ten men on the pitch.

"Come on lads" called their Captain. "We're in trouble but we can do this!"

He thought he was in trouble? He'd never even met Lurch.

But at least they weren't going to give up. Following the excitement of the chase and sending off the game quietened down. Leeds were happy to settle for the one-nil and Rotherham struggled to muster an attack. I couldn't see an opportunity to let them through. Everything was so tight all over the pitch and time was running out. With just ten minutes left there was an announcement over the loudspeaker system which was usually used to give instructions to visiting supporters or for emergency announcements – like would the owner of a red mini registration "RU 12" move it immediately as it is blocking the entrance to the lavatories. On this occasion and in the quiet of the game I heard it clearly. "Would Harry please meet Mr A. at home after the match?"

There may have been five hundred Harrys in the stadium and at least a couple of dozen Mr A's but I knew exactly which Harry the announcer was referring to. Things were getting desperate. Rotherham needed to mount an attack of some sort but couldn't get out of their own half. I trundled up to the half way line and, seeing my opportunity, put in a heavy challenge on one of their midfielders. From the ground he looked up at me and suggested that he should have let their Number 9 have me. He was right of course. The free kick gave them a chance if they took it long. They did. It dropped into the penalty area almost at the feet of our left back. Seeing my opportunity I chased towards the ball calling "Harry's ball" and whilst taking it off his foot managed to trip over and poke it towards a Rotherham player in one move. With the ball suddenly at his feet the lucky Rotherham hero managed to strike it towards goal, out of reach of our goalie who could only watch it hit the inside of the post and rebound into the net. That was a close run thing but at least Rotherham were back in the game. I took some abuse from the rest of the team but explained I had called for the ball. It wasn't my fault – I looked pointedly at the Left Back.

Goals change games but not that much. Rotherham with only ten men were quite happy to settle for a draw. There were less than ten minutes left for them to hold out and all ten men were now back in the Rotherham half whilst I was left as our only defender. How could they possibly score a second goal if they weren't prepared to come into our half? Our team were being patient and passing the ball from left to right and back across the pitch looking for an opening. I hovered in the centre-circle watching the action. The home crowd were nearly silent, anticipating a Leeds winner. The ball came to me. I chipped it long into the Rotherham penalty area hoping their goalkeeper would get it and mount an attack from the back but the idiot initially stayed on his line. Our centre-forward had timed his run perfectly. He arrived as the ball fell to the ground and took it majestically on the outside of his right foot, beating a defender with one sweep and then lined up his shot. There was nothing between him and the goal except the tardy goalkeeper who had belatedly sprinted from his line and dived at the feet of the forward. The attacker beat him with another touch from the outside of his foot and the goalkeeper, driven by his own momentum, clattered into the player bringing him down in a heap. Penalty! No doubt about it. The whistle blew and the referee pointed to the spot. There was no appeal nor a word of complaint. I stood, dumb-struck. There was almost no time on the clock. I wandered forward. Can I take it? I asked our captain. He smiled and congratulated me on my pass but no – we had a penalty taker and he was lining up his shot. I could hardly watch. In fact I didn't. I started to scan the crowd to see if I could see where Lurch was so I could make sure I ran in the opposite direction at the final whistle. Of course not watching the penalty meant that I didn't see our star player take his long run-up. I didn't see the goalkeeper dive in the wrong direction and I didn't see the ball leave the ground travelling at the speed of sound.

I also didn't see it strike the cross-bar and fly back almost to the half-way line. Not seeing it I was therefore too late to join the pack of players who, having assumed the game was as good as over, had congregated just outside the Rotherham penalty area. Almost all of the Leeds players had sunk their head into their hands when the ball had missed the target and therefore were at a disadvantage when the fleet-of-foot Rotherham boys swept up the pitch after the ball. A few of our lads began to chase them. Our goalkeeper was caught in no-man's-land between the goal and the centre-line. He didn't know whether to come forward or go back so settled for tripping over his own feet and falling to the floor. One long boot from a Rotherham player saw the ball float gracefully high over the prostrate goalie. It bounced once in our penalty area and again on the six-yard line then rolled into the goal.

I was saved!

There was no time left for us to get back into the game. I was home-free and safe. If only I hadn't let myself down a little by leaping up in the air and punching the sky with "Yes! Get in you beauty!" If only I hadn't done that then maybe I would have got away with it all. I put it down to stress. Others may put it down to me being an idiot. I can't say it was the smartest thing that I have ever done in my life but then I am not sure what was. I hoped I hadn't been noticed but I was out of luck. If half the team hadn't seen me whoop for joy they certainly saw me hugging the Rotherham players in an ecstatic expression of delight.

The final whistle blew shortly afterwards. Not only on the game but as it happened on my time with Leeds. Don was devastated. The changing room was silent and when everybody had changed and was ready to leave Don announced that they should all get on the coach but that he wanted a word with me, alone. They all left. Don asked what my antics were all about at the end of the game. I tried to persuade him that I was just confused after being chased in the game and our missing the penalty.

"I guess I just lost it" I suggested.

But Don was smarter than that. "Have you been got at?" He asked.

I looked at my feet. I nodded. I managed to drag some tears into my eyes as I told him the story. When I finally looked up I could see that he was genuinely upset. I asked for his forgiveness but he was too shocked. His face was unusually pale.

"With the referee that we had last week and now you this week..." He shook his head in apparent disbelief. "I could never trust you again, you know. You'll have to leave Leeds. I never knew football could be corrupt like this. I have learned a hard lesson. This has cost us four points and who knows what that'll mean at the end of the season?" I thought he was going to cry, too. I had to try to comfort him.

"Boss," I said "I'm sorry." Then, cheerfully. "Shall we get on the coach, Boss? It's a fair trip home and we can have a drink on the way!"

He turned from me and sadly croaked "I think it'd be better if you made your own way home. Don't come in for training tomorrow." And he left me standing alone in the changing room. I was finished at Leeds.

There's always a silver lining, though. A few seconds later I followed Don out of the stadium. As he approached the Leeds coach a scuffle erupted from within the coach. The door was open and suddenly out tumbled a bundle of men which included two security guards and a couple of the players. The guards were trying to drag somebody away from the coach. I caught sight of a Donkey-jacket and took the opportunity to hide behind a concrete pillar. After a short scuffle the players managed to get free and return to the coach. One of the security guards managed to get to his feet whilst another lay groaning on the floor. Brennan stood up and dusted off his jacket. He called after the coach as it pulled away "You tell 'im I'm looking for 'im. You tell 'im!"

It's alright, I thought. I know. Then I headed off rapidly in the opposite direction.

Staying away from the Leeds ground meant that I could also avoid the press. The local newspaper commented on my strange behaviour in the Rotherham game but largely it went unnoticed by everybody outside the club. That was policy, of course. Leeds still hoped to get a transfer fee for me and although I was tainted in their eyes my price would only go down if the rest of football knew about my little misdemeanour. Within two weeks they had arranged for my transfer to a London club – Queens Park Rangers who played out of Loftus Road in West London. It could have been a lot worse. It could have been Wales! I left Leeds to move into digs near what was becoming the centre of the swinging sixties. The King's Road, Chelsea.

As for Leeds, well the four points dropped in the Rotherham games would have seen them equal to second place Chelsea who were promoted into the top division. Rotherham did the "double" against only one other team that season – bottom placed Luton. I don't think Don ever forgave me. I am certain that he never forgot. I'd like to think, though, that he learned something from the experience and that he took that lesson forward in his illustrious career.

London Town

Although I had left Yorkshire I could continue in my position as the player's union representative at least until the next election but I had realised that the opportunities for advancement and, more importantly, profit-making in the PFA were quite limited. I had plans to move in a different direction so I wasn't too bothered at the thought of losing that job. QPR, as Queens Park Rangers continue to be known, had enjoyed a wonderful start to the season. Five wins and two draws in their opening seven games had taken them to the top of Division 3. What they needed for their push for promotion was a big, strong, quick (so far so good), skilful (well, sometimes), intelligent (I have never claimed to be that), professional to form an impenetrable barrier in front of their goal. What they got was me.

I made my debut in the local derby with South London side Crystal Palace. Sadly we lost one-nil. By the middle of October QPR had lost six out of eight games and dropped into the bottom half of the table. I was also dropped. The team managed to rally back to sixth place by the end of April but then, forced to play me due to injuries, four straight defeats finished off any hopes that they had of a promotion.

The season was unmemorable for most of the players but for me it was special because I scored a rare goal. Actually not so much rare as unique because it was the only one I ever got as a professional. It was the seventh goal of seven that put the nail in the coffin of Hinckley Athletic a strong team from the Midlands. Let me tell you about it. Don't skip this bit. With just a minute left on the clock to play and with them exhausted and six-two down I collected the ball from a tired clearance. Controlling it with my chest, I then went past two players and slammed the ball into the back of the net with the outside of my right foot. It reminded me of my childhood days and felt so good that I briefly wished I could have done it more often. That showed them hoity-toity bank clerks, builders and delivery men from the Southern League.

I came to know all the fashionable places in the West-End of London. The clubs and pubs all welcomed us footballers but the wages of a third division footballer would not meet the needs of a man-about-town like myself. Prices, when you are paying your own way rather than on expenses, were too high and I had to find another source of income. I now entered a period of my life which has remained a very close secret but these are my memoirs and so I have to tell you the whole story. You have to remember that I had little going for me except my body. I was tall and lean and, I'll be honest, very easy on the eye in a rugged, manly sort of way.

This is how it was. A few months after moving to London I found myself in a club called Samantha's somewhere near Oxford Street. It was all strobe lights, music with a good rhythm and free-spirited girls with even better rhythm. One particular young lady took my fancy and we ended up back at her place near the river in Putney. Her "pad", was fantastic. It was a very modern flat with bean-bags instead of chairs and a useful glass topped table. Everything was in the very height of 1960's fashion. There was a view over the Thames and floodlights which sparkled on the water. She went by the very trendy name of Lucinda although I think her real name may have been Susan. Lucinda had been to a top public school but had fallen out with Daddy who had wanted to protect his little darling and keep her nice and safe in the Hertfordshire countryside. When we got to her apartment I asked her what Daddy wanted to protect her from. She showed me and I reckon the old man was right, but too late. As a result of this row with her father she had been forced to find a job to subsidise her lifestyle beyond the weekly £200 pittance that Daddy was trying to make her live on.

I had an idea what she may be doing for a living but I was wrong and got my face slapped for suggesting such a thing. I didn't mind too much being cuffed because at least I was £10 better off than I thought I'd be and that led to a general bit of wrestling with the inevitable result. As it turned out £10 would have been very good value for money. Lucinda was quite an upper-class lass but in moments of weakness – and she had a few of those with me in her circular bed - I wasn't quite sure if she hadn't got some of the gamekeeper's blood in her.

Lucinda told me that she was a model who put clothes on to have her photo taken, not the kind who took them off. Not that I'd have turned my nose up if she had. It was her idea that I should give it a try. I thought I could earn a bit extra so why not?

How things had changed since my days in Leeds. I had swapped Park Lane in Leeds for Park Lane in Westminster. Whereas in my early youth a dance was something that we looked forward to for months now every night was Party Night. Lucinda liked to host and threw a small function at her home early in 1963, partly to introduce me to some of her modelling friends and partly because she liked have fun. It was there that I once again bumped into Christine. I hadn't forgotten either her or John from our meeting a couple of years earlier. Trust me – if you had met Christine you wouldn't have forgotten her either. I managed to get her attention but was devastated to find that she didn't remember me at all. It could have been a massive blow to my self-esteem, I suppose, but at the time I didn't know what an ego was so I just concentrated on trying to chat her up. She looked every bit as good as she had a couple of years earlier, wearing a low-cut red dress that started where it got very interesting at the top and ended on her bronzed thighs. Being mesmerised by this stunner I completely forgot that I was supposed to be hosting the party with Lucinda who forced me to wave her away several times as she came over to interrupt the in-depth conversation I was having with Christine just to ask me to pass around the vol-au-vents or whatever. To my surprise Christine wasn't particularly interested in me and I had to work very hard to keep the conversation on track. I assumed that was because she felt some kind of loyalty to her host so I explained that Lucinda and I weren't a couple but she told me that she wasn't bothered if men had wives in fact, she explained, all the married men that she had slept with had wives. I remember she laughed loudly at that. I was confused but it all made sense a few weeks later.

I knew I was in trouble shortly afterwards when Lucinda came over and fetched me a fierce slap across my face. I hadn't been hit so hard by a woman since I was seven and Mum had been called to school to punish me after I had been caught hiding in the shower in the girls' changing room. Dad said I deserved it for getting caught but I was just curious, that's all. I mean you go to school to learn, don't you?

It was a cold bum in bed that night. After Lucinda's fit of jealousy Christine had blanked me for the rest of the night and left with some rich-looking foreign fellow, Russian I think. Enough was enough. As lovely as she was Harry Barker could not be cast aside like…. like … well, like a girlfriend of Harry Barker's. Who did she think she was? I had been left to wander the room eventually meeting up with a friend of Lucinda's from the modelling world called Harvey. Lucinda had introduced us earlier in the evening. I decided that it may make some amends to Lucinda if I spoke to him and maybe tried to get some modelling work which, after all, was the stated purpose of the party. However I wasn't in a great frame of mind. Alright, I was sulking so rather than playing the Great Host I told Harvey the whole story about meeting Christine a couple of years earlier. I said I had fallen in love with her and that is why I had upset Lucinda but he saw through that lie, anybody would. We both knew how I felt about Christine. It was out and out unbridled lust and I was the spoiled child that had the toy that I wanted taken away from me. I told him about John and he was intrigued. He pumped me for information, a description of the man, the date, what was said and who was there and more and more. Whilst I was talking we were joined by another individual. This man, apparently a friend of Harvey's, was poorly dressed as somebody who has made a pathetic attempt to dress fashionably but simply didn't have the money or the style or the face or the physique to pull it off. I should have guessed he was a journalist. How had he got in there?

I told Harvey that I planned to get even with John if I ever saw him again. Harvey's companion simple said "Don't worry, you have", and left as a man on a mission. Harvey seemed pleased that his friend had gone. It seems I had done something to make him happy and Harvey agreed to look for some modelling work for me and we agreed that I should come to his studio. Well, I thought, at least I got something out of the evening.

You've probably heard all about the Christine Keeler and John Profumo business and how her involvement with both John, a government minister, and a Russian 'diplomat' brought the government down so I won't go into it here. All I'm saying is that if you cross Harry Barker then watch your back. That's all I'm saying.

It takes all sorts to make a world and the modelling business certainly had its share. Harvey was a man who was very much at ease with other men. He was what people these days call "gay". In those days people had a lot of other names for men like Harvey but I simply took the view that as they were no competition when it came to the ladies then whatever they did was fine by me. Always smartly dressed with a cravat tucked into the top of his shirt and the tightest of trousers Harvey had taken a liking to me. I too liked clothes and tried to keep up with the latest fashions including body-hugging trousers. Harvey expressed a great appreciation for the shape of my arse and couldn't seem to get enough of my shoulders. We talked business and he made me an offer but in the end I just took some modelling work. The customer was a famous catalogue company that employed people to take orders and deliver to people's homes and then to collect payment in the form of a few pence each week. Top of the range stuff, you can imagine.

I was asked to model suits, collared t-shirts, collarless jackets in the style of the Beatles and, with just a little bit of padding, swimming trunks. All very proper and civilised, well paying and nothing that I couldn't tell my mum about but of course it was something that I'd not want the lads back at QPR to find out about. Some of them, unfortunately, may have taken the opportunity to engage in some ribaldry and mickey-taking at my expense. You know what young men are like. So I decided it would be best to keep this sideline to myself.

Harvey was a real good laugh. He and his friend Robert, a pale faced chap in his late twenties who worked in a clothes shop in Regent Street, lived close to Lucinda and so were regular visitors. They'd always bring a bottle of wine and usually a few bottles of stout just for me. Laughing good humouredly at my "Northern Ways" and asking me about black sausage and if all Northerners were "real men" like me. The months went by and the football season progressed unspectacularly. The money coming in from modelling was much appreciated.

Lucinda had many other parties and I should mention one of them to you as, thinking back, it may have been the final straw that put a nail in the coffin of our relationship. And in those mixed metaphors you have the nub of the problem. You see things and people changed. Lucinda forgave me my little indiscretion with Christine and I tried to behave myself around other women, when Lucinda was there. But things got serious. Not between Lucinda and me but for everybody else. Instead of going to parties to have a drink and enjoy themselves and maybe pick someone up for the night people would come along and start talking about women's rights and the war in Asia and politics and the like. Well I was a professional footballer from St Runwald's School in Leeds so I ain't interested in all that stuff. What's more I hadn't had half the education that these Oxford comedians had. As far as I was concerned Homer was a referee who gave the local team the rub of the green and the Domino Effect was what put old men into pubs on a Tuesday night in Wakefield.

Being the dummy in the room started to get on my nerves and sometimes I think Lucinda felt embarrassed by me. I often had to work extra-hard in the bedroom to make sure she didn't forget why she kept me around. It was a very comfortable billet for most of the time and Lucinda's £200 per week went a long way; but even then sometimes I wondered if I was out of my depth. Like the time we were talking and one of the girls called me a sexist. Now the way I see it a guitarist plays the guitar, a typist is good at typing and an economist is interested in the economy so surely a sexist is somebody who is interested or good at sex. And that is me! You can't muck about with the English language and I still think it makes sense but it caused a bit of a row with me telling this nut-case that she was a silly little Australian girl and that if she had been getting plenty then she wouldn't be quite so upset about all these problems in the world.

I knew I had another cold bum to look forward to in the bedroom that night. As it happens Lucinda sat in bed reading a book the Aussie girl had given her called "The Feminine Mystique" which, from what she later told me, amounted to "Women Like It Too". I could have told her that. Better than that, I could have shown her quicker than it takes to read a couple of chapters.

Well on the evening in question we were having a dinner party. Lucinda had knocked up something exotic. I think it was Spaghetti Bolognaise and to go with it we had some Hungarian wine called Bull's Blood which sounded about as good as it tasted. For those of you who are unfamiliar with good wine Bull's Blood is to fine wine what blended whiskey is to a single malt but at the time I was happy to put as much of it away as I could on the understanding that the evening would pass a lot quicker if I experienced it through a haze. I also found that the more I drunk of it the wittier I became. Alcohol has that affect on me.

The guest list was packed with talent. Benny, a TV comedian, had been invited along. He was struggling to make his show a success and it showed on his face. Where we expected him to be a laugh a minute he just sat quietly and ate nervously. He wasn't drinking and seemed shy, particularly of the women. The women! What a bunch. Maybe Lucinda had learned a lesson when she allowed Christine to come to her party and had decided not to put me in the company of any more stunners. I took a good look at Mary but her husband, one Alex Plunket-Greene if I remember correctly, was very attentive. She was a bit too old for me anyway and nowhere near as attractive as Lucinda. So what would be the point? Apparently they owned a clothes shop which sold clothes that Mary designed and made so I knew straight away that they would be a real barrel of laughs. I tried a quick pun on her having us in stitches but it flew right over their heads. There were also a couple of young American actors who were over here trying their luck. One was Jim and the other was called Jerome or something. It turned out that they had been trying to break into theatre production in the States for a couple of years without any luck so they decided to try what they thought would be an easier market in London. So many Yanks got lucky over here during the war I reckon the rest of them thought the "pickin's" were easy. I didn't take to them. They kept touching me unnecessarily and asked if I had ever been to the States. Apparently I looked like a famous American sportsman but then, as one of them said, handsome, fit men with narrow waists and broad shoulders look good the world over. I didn't argue.

The meal went on forever. In China I'm told they used to have feasts that went on for days with exquisite courses being served at regular intervals by lovely girls and entertainment provided by acrobats and dancers and the like whereas we talked about the pasta and we talked about the sauce and we talked about the wine. I knew there was cheese and biscuits to follow so I looked forward to discussing the variety of cheddars currently available on the market and possibly, if we were all very, very good we could all list our ten favourite jams as the desert was served. It was tinned fruit and ice-cream. My favourite.

We ran out of the Bull's Blood early in the proceedings so I moved onto the gin. Lucinda suggested I drank a little less and, to be fair, I had taken the lion's share. But, as I remember pointing out I was the only one in the room with balls anyway so why shouldn't I drink all the wine. Bull's Blood, you see! I laughed but it seems my wit was unappreciated by this sober bunch of Presbyterians. The party was more like tea at the vicarage after burying the Pastor. Alright, I know what you're thinking. Lucinda didn't deserve that. I suppose you are right but I was a victim of the evil of drink, wasn't I?

The evening headed downhill like the sure winner of a soap-box derby so I focussed on emptying the gin bottle as quickly as possible, adding minimal tonic water to give the appearance of civilisation. Lucinda made it clear that it would be Arctic in the bedroom again that night. Ah well, I thought, I may as well get drunk so I poured myself another large one.

As I sat there silently drinking it gave the others an opportunity to air their woes. Mary, it seems, had hit a stale patch. The shop was stagnating and sales dropping. Her recent outfits had stayed on the hangers. I looked at the drab outfit that she was wearing and was about to comment when I caught a glimpse of Lucinda's eyes which lanced across the room into my own. I took another gulp from my tumbler. Hearing Mary's afflictions encouraged the American boys to throw in their troubles. They had written good, entertaining material. There was music, dancing and political comment. There was wit and pathos. Their work had everything. It was "Great Art" but still nobody wanted to give them a theatre to exhibit their masterpiece. Why? They asked the room. Why?

But surely, I answered on behalf of the four mute walls which seemed to be swaying as if we were at sea, they had just answered their own question. It was precisely because they had music and wit and Portos and Artos and probably bloody Aramis and d'Artagnan sitting on the stage pretending to be flowers that nobody would want to see their play. I may have got things a bit confused but I had been watching

Douglas Fairbanks in The Three Musketeers earlier that day on the telly in an attempt to get up to speed on the world of theatre and art. Also to try to answer a question which had confounded me since I first saw the film as a nine-year old at the "Saturday Morning Pictures" back home in Leeds. Which of the beauties in the film would I go for? The haughty Queen whose desires were bridled by the silks and corsets that her rank demanded and who clearly waited for the right man to come along to liberate her from those restraints? The healthy, free spirited servant girl who was ready to be companionable as she followed her heart and laughed and flirted openly with the men? Or the wicked woman, driven by a selfish need for power born, no doubt, from the frustration of having to maintain a level of personal control rather than to allow her passions to explode in a crazed avalanche of rampant sexual gratification. It's a difficult choice, isn't it? Of course, in later years I realised the answer is, given the choice, all three.

Somebody suggested that I was pissed so by way of denying that I lifted my glass to demonstrate that I hadn't drunk anywhere near enough to make me inebriated. At least I tried to raise my glass but only succeeded in knocking it over and spilling the contents onto the cheese plate, completely ruining two ounces of dried and cracked Red Leicester. A big fuss was made about that and white serviettes flashed around the table in a re-enactment of the Liverpool dockside at the first sailing of the Titanic.

I re-filled my glass and sheepishly sat in silence once again.

It was now Ben's turn to speak. He had hardly said a word during the evening. The short, chubby little fellow had kept his eyes fixed on the tablecloth or the plate in front of him. I think he was quite short-sighted because whenever he looked at Lucinda he seemed to have to squint in order to bring her into focus and as he did so his tongue popped out giving his face the appearance of a constipated cat straining for relief. We already knew about Ben's problem. He was a comedian and had a TV show but audience figures were dropping and although he had been given another series it was likely to be his last with the BBC unless things changed! Well I liked the fellow, he seemed to bring out the maternal instinct in the women and he didn't complaint at all when Lucinda put her arm around his head and held it closely to her breast. As I sat there I realised that if I could have helped him I would have done but I couldn't so I'd better top my glass up again.

Of course everybody wanted to help little Benjamin. Jerome proposed that he should bring other stars onto the show, perhaps some of the stars from the big West End musicals would like to get some publicity for their shows by appearing on television. It would also attract the middle and upper classes who couldn't always get up to town to catch the latest shows, James suggested. Mary thought that he could improve things by having some really interesting costumes. That'd be bound to attract a wider audience from the rag trade. This well-meaning pathetic group then went on to expand their ideas. Mary would have the show turned into a cat-walk. The Americans became excited at the thought of extracts from their shows being aired live on TV and I got annoyed because we had run out of Gin. Why wouldn't these people go home?

My head dropped forward and my eyes closed. I may have been about to nod off but then, through a haze, I received a moment of epiphany. That is to say I had a sudden James Joyce-like realisation that they were all talking bollocks and that the only person in the room with the necessary clarity of thought was Harry Barker Esquire. Everything came to me at once. Firstly I realised that they wouldn't go home until somebody had sorted out their problems for them. Secondly I realised that I held the answer and thirdly I remembered that there was another bottle of red plonk tucked away in the top cupboard. Lucinda had added some to the spaghetti bolognaise. She called it cooking wine but she wasn't fooling me. Wine is wine!

I left the table to retrieve it and caught my foot under the leg of Jerome's chair. Fortunately I regained my balance and composure by leaning on Mary's shoulder. I looked at the assembled group and, I promise you, they were all looking at me with the contempt that is usually held for the house pet that has just farted. (I had just farted as it happens but I didn't think they had heard me.)

"What are you lot looking at?" I demanded, raising myself to my full height and sticking my chest out. "You're all nothing special." I told 'em. "Look at you! A bunch of no-nothing failures. You haven't got a clue."

Lucinda was spraying an expensive perfume into the air. I never found out why.

I continued my tirade. "You sit there with your hoity-toity ways and your uppity posh lah-de-dah chit-chat about nothing but you haven't got the brains to see what's right in front of your nose."

To be fair Ben had. Lucinda was kneeling on the floor at his side trying to retrieve my glass which had somehow fallen from my hand, onto the floor and rolled under the settee. Her bum was sticking in the air as she stretched to reach it and Ben was squinting, with his tongue out, in an attempt to get a good view.

"Sex" I said. "That's what it's all about." Ben took his eyes off Lucinda's arse and looked at me guiltily. His mouth clamped shut on his tongue giving him a well-deserved nip.

"Give people what they want" I told them "and what they want is sex."

Everybody's mouth was open as they gaped at me. "You, Benny." I was being friendly. "Get girls on your show. Get 'em to take their kit off. Get 'em to show off their legs and their tits and their bums. They'll love it and the lads at home will love it too."

"Rubbish" Mary interjected.

"And you." I turned on her. "Look at that thing you're wearing. Where's the fun in that? Girls want to show off what they've got and men want to see it. Sex is what it is all about. Show off a bit of leg, that's what you need to do. What's the point in wearing clothes that cover up all the good bits?"

She wasn't impressed but I could see her husband thought it was a good idea. Jerome and Jim weren't impressed by my argument though.

"Oh!" said Jim and I suppose you expect us to have our actresses all dancing around stark naked do you?"

I nodded vigorous agreement as Jerome added "And our actors!" Jim gave him an "I'll talk to YOU later" look which immediately shut him up.

"Yes." I insisted, just as I managed to lay my hands on the remains of the cooking wine. "That's what you need to do and then ordinary people will start to take notice of you."

"And another thing." I honed in on Mary. "Who one earth wants to buy a dress off somebody called 'Plunket-Greene'? You sound like a bloody golf course. Change your name for God's sake."

"Really?" She smarmed sarcastically "And what should I call myself? Betsy Barker?"

I gave her a name but I think, looking back, she may have misheard me because I didn't say "Quant" at all – but the name worked out for her and so did the mini-skirt.

After that spat I had had enough so I announced to the gathering "You can all piss off now because I am going to bed!" and with that I took the last of the wine into Lucinda's bedroom, put it to my lips and fell unconscious onto the bed.

I am glad that Ben took my advice, though. Not just because it made him a fortune and kept him on the TV for nearly thirty years but because even I would tune in every week to hear his clever but smutty jokes and ogle at the Hill's Angels who cavorted semi-clad on our screens each week. Good for you, Benny.

As for the other two they disappeared back to the States shortly afterwards and I never heard from them again. Not unless they were that pair Gerome Ragni and James Rado who kicked up a storm with that musical "Hair" late in the sixties. I didn't mind the women singing and bouncing around the stage naked but did they have to all those fellows with their tackle dangling about? Sometimes people can take things too far.

A Brief Stroll on the Wild Side

Like I said, things with Lucinda tailed off rapidly after that night. Sometime later I think she changed her name and made a pop record and, when that phase of her life was over, married an Earl or a Lord or something. We didn't break up in a big blazing argument but sort of drifted into other things. She may have found somebody else and dumped me or I might have started sleeping with somebody else and forgot to go back to her. Either way, possibly with nowhere else to go after a night on the town, I regularly found myself waking up in the early hours of the morning on the sofa in Harvey and Robert's flat. As a sportsman I was quite used to men walking around naked in the changing rooms so I was quite comfortable with Harvey and Robert doing the same. They didn't seem to mind me doing that either although there was a hell of a row one day when Robert seemed to have got it into his head that Harvey had spent a bit more than a moment looking at my back-side. It didn't help when I explained that it was part of his job to keep an eye on my bum and that he was always checking that I was keeping it trim.

A few days later I awoke to find Harvey in tears. Robert had not come home the previous evening. Harvey believed he had met somebody else the night before. All I did was to put my arm around Harvey to comfort him. It was the first and only time I had ever done anything like that and of course the front door flew open and there was Robert in the doorway whilst I stood there naked with an arm around his lover. Robert threw a tantrum. He flounced into the bedroom and immediately began to pack. They were going to have a row so I dressed and left.

My next modelling assignment was a week later. Harvey was supervising the photographers but he looked awful. When there was a break I asked him what the problem was and he explained that Robert hadn't moved out but that he was going out alone in the evenings. Harvey was sure that Robert was seeing somebody else and he planned to follow Robert that night. He wanted me to come with him. I wasn't keen but this poor vulnerable chap was so upset and had some very lucrative modelling assignments coming up which he felt I really shouldn't miss out on so I agreed to come to his flat that evening and that we would take things from there.

Sure enough Robert left the flat around 8 p.m. He hadn't spoken to Harvey or I other than simple pleasantries such as "have you finished in the bathroom?", "You could have cleared up after yourself. It's always me that has to do it." And "Don't make me a coffee will you. Just wait for me to put the kettle on." The usual stuff. Harvey and I quickly put our jackets on and set off to follow Robert at a distance. Fortunately he did not catch a taxi, although it would have been great to jump in a cab and say "follow that car". He walked away from the Thames towards Victoria Station and as we passed the Station's main entrance Harvey whispered to me "I know where he's going. The Breaker's Club." It wasn't a club I had heard of, so I whispered back to Harvey. "I haven't heard of that club."

Harvey explained that he was quite sure I wouldn't have heard of it. It wasn't for my sort. It was for gentlemen of class and quality and certain exclusive tastes.

I understood immediately. It was a lifestyle thing. His lifestyle, not mine.

Eventually we stopped outside a thick, panelled, jet-black door which was at the top of a half-a-dozen marble stairs which in turn rose from street level. There was no sign or mark on the door which gave entrance to this early Victorian building. You either knew what was behind that door or you weren't supposed to. Harvey whispered into an intercom system and the door buzzed open. It was dark the other side of the door and impossible to see inside from the street. I followed Harvey through, more curious than nervous. The door shut behind us and Harvey pushed aside a curtain to reveal a richly decorated staircase leading upwards. He led and I followed, stunned by the sumptuousness of the surroundings.

Once at the top of the stairs he opened another panelled door, this time white, and we entered a large hall decorated with silk curtains draped over sedans, classic furniture and fashionably dressed men of all ages holding and dancing with each other. It was nothing that I hadn't seen before at Harvey's flat but I was quite taken aback by the scale. I looked a bit closer and noticed that there were a few women dotted around the room. Not many but they too were all well dressed, largely in evening gowns. There were well over a couple of hundred men in the club. Proving, beyond any reasonable doubt, that homosexuality was not as unusual as I had been led to believe. Possibly every homosexual in London was in the room. In fact, as I looked around I realised that it may be more common than I thought because dancing not more than ten yards away from me were two middle-aged Football Association officials in the arms of a pair of young First Division footballers and one of them was none other than my oily friend, Passmore, who I had last seen on my trip to Chile. The other I had seen at some PFA meetings but could not remember his name. The professional footballers I knew only from the television screen. The music paused and I strolled over to where the quartet now stood. Men nodded to me in a friendly fashion as I passed by. I smiled in acknowledgement and moved on.

Passmore initially seemed surprised to see me but then welcomed me gracefully, introducing me to the First Division players. The other FA official seemed pleased to see me too. He knew my name. I wasn't sure I liked the way he studied my physique. His companion definitely didn't like it and led him to the centre of the dance-floor for a turn. Passmore offered to buy me a drink. I was never one to turn away a free drink so asked for a pint of mild. They thought that was funny and Passmore explained that they didn't serve pints. "Just cocktails" added his companion with what may have been a meaningful look. Passmore handed me a drinks menu from which I think the only ones that could ever be mentioned in a family newspaper would be the

"White Russian" and "Black Russian." One drink I couldn't possibly mention was the "Long Slow Comfortable Screw Up against a Wall". How could I ask for one of those in that particular club? I mean. Call me naïve if you like but not an idiot!

Fortunately at that moment Harvey returned with Robert. There were tears in both their eyes and Harvey explained that he and Robert had some matters to discuss and were going to spend the evening together at the club. They wanted to be alone. I understood of course and was pleased that they were going to get things sorted out. Saying thanks and goodnight Harvey leaned forward and placed a gentle kiss on my cheek. Robert, too, hugged me. He was wearing quite a nice aftershave but I resisted the temptation to ask him which one. They crossed the room hand in hand and Passmore and his friend looked sympathetically at me and asked me if I'd like to join their group. They were going-on somewhere later. I declined. After all I wouldn't want people to get the wrong impression about me.

I was about to leave when suddenly a stunning woman stepped out of the shadows and onto a small stage in the centre of the room. Immediately the dancers stopped their cavorting, applauded her briefly and took their positions encircling her at the edge of the dance-floor. She wore a long red-dress which was split to the thigh to reveal a long, shapely, but perhaps slightly muscular leg. Her hair was raised about a foot above her head in a Bouffant style. That, plus the lift on the fine stilettos, gave her a total height in the region of seven feet. She towered over her surrounds, dominating the club with both her height and her imperious gaze with which she looked around, almost contemptuously at the proletariat who surrounded her. Regal disdain you may call it. Her eyes were outlined in thick dark mascara whilst her lips were cherry-red. Her complexion appeared smooth and creamy. The red dress had a high neck-line and hugged her shapely figure from the wide hips to the broad shoulders detouring only to accentuate large high breasts. Her arms and hands were covered by long, perfectly white gloves. I decided to take a drink and see what more this Amazon would offer. I rarely drank whiskey but felt it the safest option. Errol Flynn and Rock Hudson drank whiskey, didn't they? And you don't get any more macho than them.

This incredible creature spoke a few words of welcome whilst I was getting my drink and then lit into a wonderful song, one of the hits from a few years earlier. Her voice was low in the manner of Marlene Deitrich. The crowd loved her, applauding her every move and word. As she sang she moved over to some of the men in her audience and touched them gently on the arm, on the cheek even squeezing a thigh or two. Cheeky but I thought she was wasting her time on that lot, she was just teasing them safe in the knowledge that they wouldn't be interested in any woman, even one as striking as her - but if she came over to me and tried it – well, anything could happen. But I was too far away, on the edge of the crowd. I watched as she began a second song, moving her body rhythmically to the sway of the music. The singing wasn't brilliant but she held this audience in the palm of her hand (even literally now and then) and they lapped it up.

I was mesmerised by this dazzling spectacle and, not having taken my eyes off her, I hardly noticed the attractive young woman who was now standing next to me, occasionally, and I soon realised, deliberately, knocking against me as she moved to the music. I took a quick look and wasn't unhappy to be faced with a well-rounded, perhaps slightly plump creature with a beautiful big smile which showed off her brilliant white teeth between her full red lips. Her hair fell shoulder-length onto her bare shoulders uncovered by the full-length crimson gown that she wore. She had obviously taken a fancy to me and although my interest was quite firmly with the goddess who was on stage I decided that a bird in the hand was almost certainly worth two in the bush or, in this case the one on stage. So I carefully placed my arm around the girl's soft shoulders and offered to help her keep upright. She gave me an even broader smile and allowed herself to lean into my ample chest. We watched the show briefly before moving back to the bar together. From there we could talk and get a much better view of the entertainment. She introduced herself as Leslie if I remember rightly.

Leslie worked in a bar elsewhere in London and had come to the club with a friend, and colleague of hers. He was gay and so, as she explained, she had accompanied him to somewhere where he could feel comfortable. This club. A short while later a very handsome and well dressed young man came over to join us. This was Adam, her colleague. He was almost as tall as me and very muscular. He greeted me frostily intentionally, and successfully, making me feel uneasy. I suspect that he felt some responsibility for Leslie but she soon persuaded him that she felt comfortable with me and that she wanted to stay with me. I gave him my best winning smile and he moved away leaving Leslie with the simple instruction to "be careful". Not a problem, I thought, I'll take care of her, alright.

There were cubicles on the perimeter of the room and we managed to find an empty one which, while it didn't completely hide us from view, did give us enough cover to allow some intimacy. I prefer privacy when I am in the act of seducing somebody and Leslie had obviously fallen for me in a very big way. She clung to me and within seconds of sitting down her mouth had found my own. Her plump lips pressed onto me as her mouth opened under the mild pressure that I was applying. I have fancied myself as a bit of a good kisser but Leslie had me beat. She seemed to know exactly how to interest me in the close dance our heads were performing and her tongue flicked gently, occasionally, against my teeth and tongue. Now I know you might be wondering why I am spending so much time telling you about one simple kiss, bearing in mind that by this time I had slept with dozens of women and I haven't bored you much with the details of that. But there is a reason.

Leslie and I were clearly a good match and I knew, as I always did, that it wasn't a case of "if" but "when" and "where". My place or hers? At this particular time my "place" had tended to be either at Lucinda's flat or Harvey's couch, my own flat was a little bit further to travel. So my preference was her place. She was in favour of the idea but wasn't ready to leave yet. The little minx wanted to make me wait a bit longer. Fair enough, I thought, and fetched a couple of drinks from the bar. I was never one to ask too many details about the lives of the girls that I have slept with. Simple questions like "Are you married?" and "Do you care?" were usually the limit of my interest. In Leslie's case she wanted to hear all about me but said little about herself other than that she had come down from Birmingham alone a few years earlier. Clearly a very independent girl and experienced too. She hadn't wasted her time in the Smoke and proved it by moving her fingers inside my shirt at the first opportunity to stroke the young hair on my chest. While she did that with her right hand somehow her left found its way onto my thigh and crept higher and higher up my leg.

At that point I noticed that Harvey and Robert were standing arm in arm a few feet away from where we were sitting. Clearly they were now back together. Robert's head rested on Harvey's shoulder. I decided to have a quick word with them to tell them that I would be staying elsewhere that night. It all looked good with Leslie and I was looking forward to my just rewards for helping Harvey and Robert through a bad patch. I excused myself and extracted my body from Leslie's entwine. I pointed at Harvey and Robert and explained, as I left her in the cubicle, that I wanted to tell my friends that I was leaving the club.

Harvey and Robert were pleased to see me and Harvey greeted me with an affectionate hug. I held him off a bit because I didn't want Leslie to get the wrong idea about my relationship with them but as Harvey released me I looked over to find that Leslie had left our table and was heading across the dance floor. The show had now ended and people were dispersing across the room, gaily laughing, clearly having enjoyed the act.

"I'm leaving with her." I told the pair, pointing towards Leslie as she moved through the room.

"Really?" Questioned Harvey. He looked surprised, as did Robert.

"Yes." I assumed they thought she had dumped me. "She has probably gone off to the Ladies."

"Ladies?" Robert smiled. "But Harry, there isn't a 'Ladies' here. This is a 'Gentlemen-Only' club."

It was my turn to look surprised. The first thought I had was very unpleasant but then I carefully thought it all through again. Only a woman could kiss like that (I told you about it, didn't I?) and the way she aroused me - it would only be possible for a highly sensual woman to do that. What a girl that Leslie was! She had fooled everybody here into thinking that she was a man dressed as a woman, when all along she was a woman after all. Brilliant! I smiled and considered telling Leslie that I knew what she had done to Harvey and Robert and everybody else there but I decided not to spoil her fun. No. I wouldn't tell on her. I'd let her carry on with her little deception. It would be our little secret.

I didn't say another word to Harvey or Robert. I just touched them gently on their shoulders, gave them the thumbs up and indicated with the same thumb that I was leaving.

Once out of the club I set off for one of my regular haunts where I drank half-a-dozen pints and picked up a girl to take back to my flat. I decided to do the same every night for the next week. Don't ask me why. I just wanted to. OK?

Downhill

As they say these days it was time to give Harvey and Robert "some space" so I kept away from their flat and saw Harvey only during the modelling assignments. The modelling work kept coming in for a while but when it eventually dried up I found myself a little short of cash each week. I wasn't playing much first team football so there were no win bonuses to help bring my income up to the level required to keep the flat and to pay for the stylish clothes to which I had become accustomed. Not to mention the clubbing and the price of drinks in London's very fashionable West-End. I therefore found myself getting into a bit of debt. I borrowed from Harvey, who didn't seem to mind. I borrowed from some of the lads at the club, who did seem to mind and persistently reminded me of the debts, with menaces. I didn't take a great deal of notice of their attempts to pressure me into paying up. In my time I had been threatened by <u>real</u> professionals.

Between you and me I may have helped myself to the occasional bits of cash that some of the players left lying around the changing room in the pockets of their trousers. Things were getting tough. It didn't help when a girl, Lucy I think her name was, turned up pregnant and claiming that I was the father-to-be. She wanted a couple of hundred pounds to pay for some medical expenses. I was usually very careful but I reckoned I'd slipped up that time. She claimed I was the first and only one. Well she would, wouldn't she? She thought I loved her. Like I said - she would, wouldn't she? I'm sure I did love her on the night but nothing's forever. I suppose she was a sensible girl really because there was no nonsense about keeping the baby. I had to do something though and decided to go back home to see Mum and, maybe, renew some acquaintances. Desperate times called for desperate measures.

You know, the saying about things having to get worse before they get better? Codswallop isn't it? Why do things have to get worse? Why can't they just get better and better? I am sure there are people out there earning vast amounts of interest on unearned income having to search daily for ways to spend it before the tax-man tracks it down. For me things got worse. I turned up at Mum's. She had no money, of course, but she did have some news. A big fellow in a donkey jacket, she thought his name was "Ben Ann" but her hearing was never very good when she had been drinking, had been turning up occasionally and asking after me. "Could she give him an address in London to find me?" Not so likely. The last thing I needed was for Brennan to be chasing me through the cobbled streets of London with, no doubt, murderous intent. Whatever he wanted could wait. I had more pressing problems.

I found what I was looking for where I had left him. Brian was leaning against the bar in the snooker hall. I dug deep and found enough to buy a couple of pints. We were both on hard times but Brian was prepared to get a message to Mr A. to tell him that I was back in town and open for business. A couple of days later a deal had been struck. Mr A. had advanced me a £500 retainer. It was to cover expenses. I told him prices were high in London. The money was for payments to people who would be helping to make sure results went our way. Alright I'll spell it out. The plan was that I was going to use my contacts in the game to fix a few results but firstly I was going to have to take £200 out of Mr A.'s bundle to pay for Lucy's abortion. There'd be a further £150 to pay off some debts, although Harvey could wait, and with the rest I reckoned I'd be able to fix up a couple of friends to throw a match or two and give Mr A. a bit of a return on his investment. There, I've said it. I never said I was an angel and I'm not expecting a knighthood (or at least I wasn't then.)

Lucy took the money and I never saw her again. Some things are not meant to be. I paid off my debts which meant I could show my face around the training ground without receiving threats of violence. I then 'phoned Uncle Vic.

I don't want to spoil a good story by going into too many details. Suffice it to say that things went well for a while. I dropped Uncle Vic a few quid and he let me know where Mr A. should put his money. It was a lot easier to make a phone call to Uncle Vic and send him £50 than it was to approach and try to bribe players myself. I also stuck a few bob on each game myself so managed to balance my books. Looking back I knew it couldn't carry on but before I had managed to get any kind of wedge behind me the whole sorry mess broke into the newspapers in what you may know as the "1964 Betting Scandal" but what I knew as the "1964 life-threatening near-bloody disaster". It was very late in the season when the story hit the press. I woke one Sunday afternoon to noise of the persistent shrill ringing of the 'phone. There were none of those fancy ring-tones in those days. It was a bell that would wake the dead – or in my case the near-dead as I'd been out clubbing the night before and taken on board what felt like enough alcohol to satisfy a plane-load of Glaswegians on their way back from Magaluf. I had a terrible moment of fear that I'd lost the use of my legs but it was only that the tart I had slept with had lain across my thighs all night and my calves had gone to sleep. Anyway I got to the 'phone as quickly as I could, mainly to stop the infernal noise from splitting my head apart. My flat was what they call a studio flat which means just one big room with sectioned areas so you couldn't even close a door between your sleeping quarters and the rest of the house.

Uncle Vic was at the end of the line, the other end I mean. He was shouting something about the newspapers and blubbing about "We'll all go to jail." I had no idea what he was talking about so I said "I've no idea what you are talking about."

"Right." he said "You're right. The 'phone might be bugged. Who are you anyway? This is a wrong number." And the 'phone slammed down.

"He's gone mad" I thought and went back to bed. I couldn't sleep though, and the tart wouldn't wake up despite my attempts to interest her in an action replay. So I got up and made a cuppa and a bit of toast. I decided that it'd be good to read the Sunday scandal sheet with my breakfast (or lunch or whatever meal time it was). With a mouthful of toast I picked the rag up from where it had fallen inside the front door. It lay crumpled and slightly torn on the floor having been squeezed carelessly through the letter box by our paper-boy who would have already checked through the pages for pictures of scantily clad girls and read the football reports. As I straightened it I caught the front-page headline and choked on the dry toast spilling hot tea over my naked belly and beyond. That'll be sore for a while, I thought as I charged towards the bathroom clutching the scalded area. The noise had woken sleeping beauty, who looking up and seeing me running towards her screaming and holding my dick gave an unconvincing squeal of terror herself. I bet she was disappointed when I ran straight past her to the bathroom sink to pour cold water over my genitals. I am guessing that she was further disappointed to see the shrunken result. Cold water has that effect, you know.

The news was that somebody had spilled the beans, and I am not talking about breakfasts here. The Christmas before I had even got involved there had been a bit of a fix up for a Sheffield Wednesday game against Ipswich. Wednesday would have probably lost the game anyway but nobody wants to take chances where serious money is involved so a few of the players agreed to take care of the result. Not a problem until, for some crazy reason, 18 months later somebody gets a rush of the "honesties". Not so much a case of clearing his own conscience more a case of clearing his debts, I should think. The 'papers would have paid him a fair bit to "reveal all".

This couldn't have come at a worse time for me. I had lost all my "rainy day" money betting on another sure thing just a few weeks before. Sonny Liston, the bear, the un-defeat-able World Heavyweight boxing champion had been whipped by that gangly, big-mouth kid, Cassius Clay. It had to be a fix. What was the world coming to? You couldn't trust anybody. There was going to be a re-match and I seem to remember saying to the lads at the club that they could put every penny they had on Liston in the re-match. Then that'd be the last we'd hear about Cassius Clay. I was nearly right. Clay changed his name to Muhammad Ali.

I read the newspaper story through very carefully. There were references to associates and other footballers but my name was not mentioned at all. Uncle Vic was the only person who knew of my involvement and I reckoned he would keep me out of things if he could. Only he and I knew that he was feeding me information about fixed matches. Nobody else, particularly not Brian and Mr A.

This cheered me up and the girl on the bed began to look tempting again. She seemed to be posing in a provocative style, lying on her front with her knee raised, similar to what First Aiders call the recovery position. I had fully recovered from the scalding and from the shock of the newspaper story and admired how the girl's position showed off the curve of her hips and the roundness of her back-side. Her soft breathing gently raised and lowered her profile. She was definitely encouraging me; or alternately she may have been fast asleep and oblivious to the naked giant approaching her. I was about to leap back into bed with lascivious intent when a small nagging doubt which had been flickering in the recesses of my mind suddenly burst into a searing flame. With Uncle Vic exposed and out of the picture how was I going to balance things with Mr A.?

I know what you're thinking. Why not just give Mr A. a call and tell him that all bets are off because of the newspaper story? Well the problem was that Mr A. had been feeding me cash on a regular basis to bribe players to fix games. But I hadn't been using his money for that. I'd been paying Uncle Vic some small sums for information and spending the rest on my lifestyle. If Mr A. found out that I'd been misusing his funds he wouldn't be too pleased. In fact he'd be violently upset. Another small problem was that I should have been holding around £500 of Mr A.'s money in order to fund future payments. If I told him the deal was off he'd want that money back straight away and most of it had been lost or spent on my lifestyle. A lifestyle, I may add, which at this very moment had woken up and taken herself off to the bathroom to dress. I had something to ponder but meanwhile the best thing I could think to do was to get back in bed to try to sleep off the hangover. So I did.

As if I didn't have enough problems I was called in to see the manager at QPR the following morning after training. We were coming near to the end of the season and I had only played for the first team three times. In January, when we had lost at home to Southend United, we had scored four but conceded five. I must take the blame for a couple of the goals conceded but I think it unfair to blame them all on me! Likewise the two games against Coventry City. We had scored three and conceded six at home in November then on the previous Saturday we'd played away and only let in four – but scored 2. He hadn't got a problem with my general behaviour and approach to training but couldn't see a place for me in the future of the club. I tried to argue that whilst the team had leaked fifteen goals in the three games that I had played the team had scored seven. Surely that told him something. "Yes." He replied "That no matter how many goals we score when you are playing we'll let in more." Looking back that was a pretty unkind thing to say to a lad of just twenty-one. I am not saying he was wrong because I have always been realistic about my ability. It's just that he could have put it to me a bit more kindly. Anyway he explained that he would have to release me. I was on the transfer list. I would be twenty-two at the start of the next season. I was still quick and getting stronger. Defenders improve with age. I was fairly confident of finding another club.

Battersea Park

Well the weeks went by. The season ended unspectacularly with QPR finishing around mid-table. There had been no interest shown in me so I determined to enjoy the summer, keep myself fit and keep away from my contacts in the North. The good news was that although people had been arrested for the match-fixing scandal my name still hadn't been mentioned. Mr A. had no reason to require my services – in close-season I couldn't fix matches that weren't being played – and QPR were still paying me a moderate weekly wage.

Around this time I took to running through the parks. This was mainly to keep my fitness up but also to take in the sights. A little tip for you, lads. You don't have to go to discotheques and clubs to meet girls. They go out during the day too and where better to meet them than the wide open spaces of London's grass parks? If you see a dog, then pet it. Girls love a man who loves animals. I came across a great looking girl whilst running in Battersea Park, South London. I had stayed overnight with one of the Crystal Palace lads that I knew from the PFA. She was one of those Scandinavian looking types with legs that went all the way up and a skirt that could have passed for a handkerchief. Mary had taken things a bit further than the mini-skirt and introduced the micro-mini-skirt. Quite satisfactory from where I was standing, I can tell you! There was another girl with her but I had eyes only for the blonde. As I approached them I saw my opportunity in the shape of a young black and white mongrel dog which was wandering aimlessly nearby. I lowered my body and pretended to offer the dog something to eat. "Here, boy" I called.

The stupid mutt came forward keenly. His tail wagged in anticipation. As he got close enough to me I took hold of his collar to hold him steady and stroked his head and body with my other hand. The dog was sniffing for the imaginary food. "Is this your little dog?" I called out to the girl using my most charming voice "He's a fine little fellow, isn't he?" She took the bait and came over to take a closer look. From my kneeling position I could admire the full extent of her long legs. "No, he's not mine. Do you think he's lost?" She added in a concerned voice.

What you need with a girl is a conversation opener. It was time to get up and look her in the eyes. I did, and she looked back not unappreciative, I suspect, of my superb condition. Remember that as a young man (and I'm not bragging here) I had the kind of body that would make a Greek God reach for the Bullworker and diet supplements. I then engaged her in the usual mindless trivia that one does in these circumstances. Was she local? Did she come to the park very often? Oh yes, and her name and telephone number. Having achieved my objective I thought it best to let her return to her friend whilst I set off in the opposite direction, keen to demonstrate my fitness. The only problem was that the dog was intent on being rewarded for acting as my stooge. The little idiot chased after me, yapping and snapping at my heels. After about 30 yards he ran directly into my path, twisting my ankle as my foot landed and bringing me forcefully to the ground. The morning's work was un-done as I cursed and took a swing at the little git, sorry, dog only to notice, in the corner of my eye, that the blonde had watched the whole incident. The dog stood a yard away and stared straight into my eyes. Looking back I reckon he was recording my face with the intent of getting his own back. Well two of us can play at that game, fella!

A short distance away a slim black cat suddenly dropped out of a tree. The dog saw Mrs Tibbs, or whatever, and, as the cats feet touched the ground, set off in chase as. Take care, little mutt, take care. I hobbled away, cursing.

As the new football season approached I was disappointed not to have been offered a contract by another football club. Bradford Park Avenue had inquired about me but they were the only club to have shown an interest. They had little money to spend and were lucky to stay afloat each season. The last thing I wanted to do was to go back up North. There were too many people up there who wanted to see me but that I didn't want to see. I began to be concerned about my future. Fortunately the Devil takes care of his own.

I turned up for pre-season training with QPR but my services were not required. I had never been too popular amongst the players there, especially since I had borrowed money from some of them and had found it difficult to pay them back also there were unfounded accusations that I had stolen money from some of them. Unfounded I say because they had no evidence that would stand up in court. The boss told me to make myself scarce but to keep fit just in case they could talk somebody into giving me a chance.

 QPR were obliged to pay me my wage regardless of the fact that I was not playing or training with them but it was not enough to run the lifestyle that I was used to. I moved out of my West-End flat into cheaper accommodation in South London. I could still travel quickly into the West End for the clubs but the environment was much less salubrious and I wasn't particularly proud of my single room, or my neighbours who often criticised me for walking naked to and from the shared bathroom. Old habits die hard and there was nothing about my body that the world wouldn't benefit from seeing more of. Not at twenty-one anyway.

One good thing about moving from the West End was that Brian and Mr A.'s friends would not be able to find me. I still owed Mr A. a lot of money but I couldn't give him what I hadn't got. Any reasonable person would see that. The trouble is that Mr A. didn't get to where he is (and probably remains to this day) by being reasonable.

I went to Battersea Park two or three times a week hoping to bump into the Scandinavian looking girl again. She hadn't answered the phone messages that I had left with her mother but I was confident that if I met her face-to-face I could talk my way around the little misunderstanding about the dog. I never saw her again but was quite pleased one Saturday morning to come across that same scruffy little black and white animal. I think he recognised me and watched me as I ran by. For sheer devilment, and with a plan to get my own back, I picked up a stick, waved it from side to side and threw it a short distance. Instinct meant the dog could no more stop himself from racing to pick it up than he could have from scratching a flea on his back. Like a chump he trotted back with the stick held in his mouth. I ignored him until he dropped it near my feet. Then I snatched it up and threw it once more. He chased and returned it. Behind me I could hear the ducks chortling in the lake. Now for Phase II of my plan. I wandered over towards the lake and once again waved the stick in the air mesmerising the waggie-tailed mutt. He was enjoying it, so far. This time, before I threw it I waved it close to his mouth, provoking him to try to snatch it from me. Then I pretended to throw the stick once more, but held on to it. He chased a half a dozen paces before returning. His head cocked to one side. I waved the stick and pretended to throw it once more. The same happened but he took fewer steps. I repeated this process a few more times as gradually the dog became more and more frustrated. Then, the coup-de-grace. I waved the stick, pretended to throw it then held it up in the air. The dog had caught on and made no attempt to follow the stick until I had finished my move. He then sprinted towards me and leapt into the air trying to grab it from my hand. I whipped it out of the way like a matador's cloak and saw the dog flying past me into the filthy water of the lake. The ducks laughed their approval of his graceless entry into their domain. Eventually the sodden mutt broke to the surface and coughed out a mouthful of stale water. I ran off smiling as he began to swim to shore. One all!

Park Avenue

A few days into the New Year I received two disturbing letters which called me Northward. One was from Mum. She was unwell and wanted me to return home to see her. This was very unusual because Mum was the strong one in our family. Dad had been away for a few years now so Mum had been living alone. It's funny that in all the years I spent at home there were always relatives, uncles and cousins who visited regularly but over the last four or five years the visits seem to have dried up. I didn't want to go back but if Mum wanted me I had better make the journey. Never say "No" to your Mum!

The second letter was from QPR and in a way it fitted perfectly with the first. They wanted me to go for a trial with Bradford Park Avenue. That was the only club that had showed an interest in me and QPR could not keep paying the wage of a non-playing player. It was Park Avenue or nothing. I had not mentioned to anybody my trial there as a youth and thought it quite likely that the people at Park Avenue had forgotten all about me. This "trial" would be a complete waste of time though. I had no intention of ever playing for Bradford Park Avenue and I doubted that they would want me but I could visit Mum whilst I was nearby and my travel expenses would be paid so I decided not to create waves. I gave her a call to let her know I would be up to Leeds shortly.

I travelled by train two days later, dropped my luggage off at home, that is to say Mum's home, and went to visit Mum. She was in hospital and the doctors were concerned. It seems that she was suffering from a number of illnesses. Her liver was in poor condition and her chest was painful, she was being sick and was feverish. The least of her problems was the sore throat. I thought nothing of it when I woke up the following morning with a sore throat myself.

I had to be in Bradford the following day for my trial so decided to stay at home rather than walking the streets and risking meeting one of my old associates – Mr A., for example. I left the curtains closed and turned on the TV. I was dozing in the chair during the afternoon when I was woken by loud rapping on the door. I jumped up in a panic, my heart pounding like a steam train. You see as I had slept I had been dreaming of a certain married woman that I had a brief relationship with in London. So the rapping on Mum's front door had come into my dream as her old man turning up unexpectedly. I sat up-right in silence hoping whoever it was would go away. The bloody TV was still on and it suddenly blared out an advert for soap powder. Great. I thought. "Able to removed bad stains such as blood and sweat." I'll remember that! The outsider had heard the TV and rapped on the door again. I crept across the floor to the front window. If I could just move the curtain slightly to the left, I thought, I would be able to take a peek outside to see who it was. I raised my eyes to the level of the front window and with one finger hooked the curtain a fraction of an inch to the left. I could see who it was alright because just at that moment Brennan was attempting to look through the same small gap that had appeared in the curtains. He worked it out immediately that the person most likely to be surreptitiously peeking out of that window would be me. He let out a bellow and banged once more on the front door "I know you're in there! I want a word with you!"

Not so likely, thinks I, and I was into the kitchen and out of the back-door before the front had stopped shaking. Fifty yards away I could still hear Brennan pounding on the front door. Two hundred yards later I eased to a brisk walk. My throat was pretty sore by now and I had begun to feel decidedly unwell. It could have been related to the fact that I had been rudely awoken from a deep sleep and that I was wandering the streets on a January morning without a coat. Mum would have something to say about that! It was nearly visiting time at the hospital so I thought I'd go to see Mum and come back later for my luggage, then scoot off to Bradford. I had left the back-door open and the TV on. In those days you could do that where I lived and fully expect everything to be there when you returned. Not because our neighbours were fantastically honest but because people around there had nothing worth stealing.

When you are a big-time football star then you have to accept that there is a public interest in your whereabouts. I was the nearest thing that our street had got to a celebrity so, as was explained to me later, when Mum told the neighbours that I would be coming home word got around and, before one knew it, everybody who had an interest knew that I was back. That list included Mr A. who, having failed to make contact with me for the last six months or so, now felt concerned that an investment and a source of income had been lost to him. As a businessman he set about retrieving the situation that is his investment and, in short, me!

Mr A. and his entourage had been on the way to Mum's to collect me when they saw Brennan beating at the door. Anticipating my escape route they had the foresight to drive around the corner just in time to see me legging it down the street. The limousine cruised silently up behind me and as he rolled down the window Mr A. quietly asked me if I would like a ride.

Now I know you would probably have expected me to sprint off as fast as I could because to get in that car could have been to sign my own death warrant but the fact is I felt awful. Cold but feverish and exhausted. There was no point trying to out-run the Limo and Mr A.'s henchmen, two of which sat comfortably in the warmth of the leather-seated vehicle, would easily have caught me.

I just nodded and as the car stopped Mr A. opened his door at the rear of the car and I got in. Mr A. noted that I was sweating. I bet he thought it was from fear. It wasn't.

As I said Mr A. was a businessman and no fool. He had seen the newspaper reports of the "1964 Betting Scandal" and had no more interest in going to prison than the rest of us. He was grateful, he explained, that the court cases had been heard and he and I were untouched by it. It was sensible to temporarily put a stop to our "investments" in this area whilst there is a lot of public interest. I had "done well" he smiled. At that point I thought I was going to get away with it but then Mr A. wondered if I could let him have the remaining invested funds back. Not, as he explained, because he desperately needed a thousand pounds but because he had accountants who were fussy about such matters and like to keep the books straight.

"A thousand pounds?" I asked.

"Yes" he explained. "I don't really understand the arithmetic. It's just what the accountants tell me. Compound interest, exchange rates, incidental expenses etcetera, etcetera. I am sure a bright lad like you will understand, though.." he raised his eyebrows leaving the trailing sentence to await a reply.

I just nodded but he was right. I did understand very well indeed. The debt was whatever Mr A. said it was.

This kindly man then offered to drop me off at the hospital and as he let me out of the car he looked up at me and added "Look after your Mum, Harry my boy. You only have one Mum and that's something that money can't buy." I began to think he was human after all, until he continued "Not like your arms and legs and eyes. You have two each of them, don't you? For now." And the door slammed shut. I had got the message.

Mum was no better and my visit with her was cut short by the nursing staff who insisted she should rest. To show you how concerned I was I completely forgot to chat up a particularly attractive young Sister and hardly noticed her crisp authoritarian approach and how the uniform hugged the top of her thighs as she briskly marched around the ward.

The other thing that shocked me was that, as I was leaving, I had to step quickly into a side-passage to avoid meeting Brennan who was entering the hospital and carrying a large bunch of flowers. I wondered who he could be visiting but realised that this gave me a great opportunity to get home, get packed and catch a train to Bradford. I'd find somewhere to stay when I got there.

The next morning I arrived at the Bradford Park Avenue ground quite early. I wanted to get this over with as quickly as possible. I felt a bit better but my throat was quite painful and I was sweating profusely. Park Avenue, as they were known, were having a good start to their season and had been in the top two of Division Four for months. Promotion looked to be a near certainty and with that there would be financial salvation for a club that had danced with dissolution for several seasons.

Having been let into the ground and shown the same, but even more dilapidated, changing room by a young trainee I changed into my kit and put on a blue tracksuit. The only one I had. I then sat and shivered in the corner of the room. One by one the other players arrived. Several of them ignored me but a few nodded in my direction, not unfriendly but hardly welcoming. Perhaps they were preoccupied with their current situation. Money was tight. They were on low salaries. They had a chance of promotion but had only managed a draw against Notts County the previous weekend. There were two hard games coming up. Away to Rochdale then away to Newport County. This was the serious end of the season and these results could make or break their push for promotion.

I was happy to be ignored and to sit quietly in the corner, coughing and spluttering and nursing my throat. This was probably a good thing as after the training session the same young trainee told me that they had heard of my reputation as a big-mouth and the other players were pleased that I had showed a bit of humility and some respect. Humility is alright, I told him, but if he had any intention of making something of himself as a footballer he should get out of Bradford as soon as he could. I advised him to "show people what you can do and then take the first offer out of here." Nice lad. Hector was his name and he did alright for himself once he left Bradford.

I wasn't too disappointed when, as I changed back into my day suit the coach came to me and thanked me for coming along, telling me that they would be in touch with QPR. I knew I hadn't played particularly well so I thought I could predict the result. Sometimes during the practise session I found myself pondering my problems with Brennan, Mr A. and Mum. If the people there had forgotten my trial as a youngster I hadn't. I owed them a payback and if I could have caught and clobbered one of their players in the practise match I would have done. As it was I couldn't catch anything, as I found out later they, on the other hand, could.

I decided it was best to return to London that evening rather than spend more time in Yorkshire. By the time I got home I was ready for bed, which is where I could be found three days later suffering from the same vomiting that Mum had. Not only that I was covered in a red rash, my throat was on fire and my tongue covered in white spots. When I eventually was seen by a doctor my illness was diagnosed as Scarlet Fever. The good news is that a week on penicillin saw me back on my feet. Little did I know, at that time, that during my brief trip to Yorkshire I had been infected with the Scarlet Fever bacteria when visiting Mum and then passed it on to Mr A. and his car-load. Then in the dressing room at Park Avenue I had passed it on to half a dozen of the first team players. A weakened Park Avenue team narrowly lost three of their next four games. Six points lost (two for a win in those days), four of which would have made the difference between them finishing, as they did, in seventh place and being promoted. Perhaps, were it not for my visit, the whole future of the club would have been different and maybe they would not have been kicked out of the league in 1970 having finished bottom for three years on the trot.

I call that even.

Inside the FA

QPR wanted to terminate my contract but had no cause to do so and, as I was still active in the PFA – the player's union, they had to treat me with kid gloves. But I was still on a small salary and things could not carry as they were. Mr A. had made his position quite clear. Mum was quite safe from Mr A. Threatening women and children was not how people up there worked. Not like the London gangsters. It was a close community in Yorkshire and in those days everybody knew each other. I, however, would be fair game for Mr A.'s thugs.

It was time for Plan B.

Some concocted business caused me to visit the Football Association's London office in Lancaster Gate. It was, and is, a wonderful building which reeks of tradition in a way that only decades of immobility can achieve. It is an ideal home for an organisation which is steeped in the treacle of tradition and inactivity. I made an appointment to speak with Pemberton. He wasn't keen and I had to ask his secretary if it would be easier if I contacted him at home. The message must have got through to Pemberton and a date was fixed. "Tomorrow" I explained to the Secretary "was good for me." It transpired it was also good for Pemberton.

If you have an interest in football and if you have got this far into the story then I would assume you have, then you may already know that in the Year of Our Lord Nineteen Hundred and Sixty-Six the World Cup Finals were to be played in this Green and Pleasant Land. With a little over a year to go I was convinced that there must be plenty of work that was needed to be done to prepare and run the event. Work that I could certainly assist with being an experienced player, a Players Football Association Officer and somebody with experience of attending, as an official, a World Cup event ("You do remember Chile in 1962 don't you, Mr Pemberton? I wonder if you have ever spoken to Mrs Pemberton about your time there.")

Indeed somebody with my experience and knowledge would be invaluable to the Football Association at this time. Pemberton agreed. "There was," he explained, "a potential problem."

Nothing, I felt, that he couldn't overcome, surely?

The problem was that all appointments had to be agreed with the Senior Administrative Manager. A certain Mr Passmore who, Pemberton noted, was also in Chile and may not have the same positive opinion of me that Mr Pemberton had.

How surprised was Pemberton when we met with Passmore? How warmly did Passmore greet me and how readily did he find a most suitable opportunity? We all agreed that the exact responsibilities would have to be defined at a future date, of course, but a generous salary was agreed – recognising that I would have to give up both a most promising football career and my responsibilities with the PFA, you understand, and that Queens Park Rangers would be most disappointed to lose me. Also we agreed that travel would be extensive so an expense account would need to be set up immediately.

How wonderful it is to have forward thinking friends!

Having reached this understanding with my new colleagues at the Football Association I agreed termination notice from QPR, a few weeks' wages, and dropped a note to the PFA. I doubt either organisation was particularly despondent at losing me.

Mum

Things were looking slightly up. I still couldn't pay Mr A. back but at least I had a decent income and provided I never returned to Yorkshire things would be fine. As well as that I had the World Cup to look forward to. Think about all those tickets that would need to be sold! Each one at a premium! I should be able to do a wholesale deal with somebody. There'd be plenty of opportunity to make a killing and maybe I'd make enough to pay Mr A. back before he made a killing (see I was so positive I could even joke about that!)

The next year passed in a whirl. There really was a great deal to do to prepare for the World Cup Finals and I busied myself visiting grounds to check their preparedness, sleeping in interminable meetings on trivial subjects like hotel accommodation and programme printing and advertisements. I always pricked up my ears when people talked about ticket allocation though. I managed to move back from South London to a flat in the West End during this time. Possibly a mistake as Passmore found the opportunity to pop round a few times unexpectedly to see if I was interested in a night out, or a night in. In case you are wondering, I wasn't.

Mum's health improved a little but she spent a great deal of time being treated in hospital. I managed some fleeting visits, never staying more than a few hours and never letting Mum know I was coming. That was the only way I could be sure that Mr A. would not be waiting for me. As for Brennan he had visited Mum several times. Usually he would stop for a cup of tea. I had to admire his style. He was playing a canny game – keeping on Mum's good side and waiting for me to make a mistake.

I was shocked one morning to receive a call from Mum's neighbour. Mum had been taken ill again and the neighbour thought I should come to see her very soon. I understood what this meant and left for

Yorkshire the following morning. Fortunately I was in time to see Mum before she went. We spoke a little and she told me of her will.

How deep is the despair of an empty home full of childhood memories and the realisation that you are, and always will be, alone?

Later that evening I stood in the front room looking around at the remnants of Mum's life. There was a quiet knock at the door. Probably a neighbour, I thought, and opened the door without my usual caution. Brennan stood there, his broad shoulders slightly lowered but as imposing as I had ever seen him. He didn't wait to be invited in but stepped across the threshold as if he had right of way. I had no more chance of stopping him than I would have of stopping a 40 tonne truck.

"I've been looking for you" he growled "but you've been giving me the run-around. It's about my Doreen."

I thought it might be "I never touched her!" I cried out, and it was almost true.

"I know." He said. "But that ain't the point. She's a good Catholic girl and you were up in her bedroom. All the neighbours know it and she's got her reputation to think of."

Reputation, thinks I. Did he know her reputation?

"She ain't got a mum." He had obviously heard about Mum and suddenly realised what he had said. "Sorry. What I mean is that I'm the only one she has got and I have to look after her. I'll make a cup of tea. "

He put the kettle on and fixed up the teapot. He knew his way around the kitchen so I calculated that he had done this before. Him and Mum? Surely not. Mum wasn't like that. For some reason he got out three cups.

"She's a good girl, my Doreen, and she likes you. I can't do a lot for her. I'm just a working man" he explained "but I'll do the best I can for her."

He gave me a meaningful look which told me that I was considered "the best he could do." He was probably right.

I sat on Mum's kitchen chair and watched him pour out three cups of tea. Having done that he went to the front door and returned with the damsel in question. Doreen entered shyly wearing what would be her best clothes. Her face was daubed with make-up and her lipstick a bright red. Her eyes were darkened with mascara. I hadn't seen anything like it since the Breaker's Club. She leaned over and kissed my cheek.

"Hello Harry. I am sorry about your Mum."

I gave her my best half-smile back. There was nothing more that I could do. I was beaten.

Brennan and Doreen allowed me to talk about Mum for an hour or two. I told them about how she had helped me with getting into football – not the story I have just told you of course – and how she had always been behind me, encouraging me to believe in myself and all that. And so much of it was true. Time passed by and of course they could not travel home that night. It seemed a sensible thing for them to stay over. I didn't mind if Doreen made up a bed for herself in Mum's room. I slept in my own room and Brennan made do with the settee – which you'd probably call a couch. I had trouble sleeping and felt deeply unhappy so when, in the middle of the night, Doreen crept as softly as she could into my room and snuck into bed with me I didn't turn her away – it was very dark, you understand.

And when she put her arms around me and held me close to her (I have to say it) enormous bosom I let her do it - remember I was very unhappy.

And when the warmth of her body and the softness of her flesh aroused me I didn't move away – remember like most men I have two brains - one on my head and the one in charge which hangs between my legs.

And when she took advantage of that by moving herself onto me I allowed nature to take its course. And now I come to think of it, it wasn't too bad at all.

I awoke alone. Brennan and Doreen were downstairs. Doreen was tra-la-la-ing merrily as she made breakfast. The food may as well be used. There are things you have to do at times like this and I did them. "Making the arrangements" they call it. I needed to get a message to Dad, but I didn't know where he was. As Brennan and Doreen prepared to leave, Brennan, completely unaware of the event in my room during the night, gave me a very meaningful look and added "we'll see you soon."

I nodded agreement. What else could I do? Doreen enveloped me in her arms and pecked me on the cheek before lumping out of the house. Thinking back she smiled in a very satisfied way. Almost Madonna-like.

Having arranged things the best I could I left Leeds later that afternoon, taking just a box of Mum's personal things with me. That was all that I would keep. I wasn't sure how long it would take before Mr A. caught up with me. I was very careful on the day of the funeral to keep myself very much in the open. Mr A. wouldn't touch me in the full glare of a church service and burial and I left Leeds immediately afterwards with no intention of ever returning. All my ties with my home town were cut except for the pesky solicitor who wanted me to go through Mum's will with him. I had arranged for all her belongings to be sold off through a local "House Clearance" business as the council were keen to move another family into what had been our family home for three generations. Good luck to 'em.

Jules Rimet

The World Cup finals were fast approaching. No they weren't. They were approaching at the same rate they had been for the last year it was just those of us that were charging around trying to get everything organised who felt time was flying by. I bet there were schoolboys and working men all over the country, maybe the world, for whom every day felt like a fortnight and the finals seemed forever away. Time is relative. It was good for me to be busy. The solicitor, Mr Steele, the senior partner of Steele, Hyde and Hope had tracked me down to my flat and was sending me letters every week, asking me to come to Leeds to read the will with him. You'd think that if he'd managed to pass all those exams to become a solicitor he'd be able to read it for himself!

Something else was nearing crisis point. Mr A., possibly now realising that I had no intention of returning to Leeds had also somehow tracked me down to my flat in London. He wasn't the sort of fellow to drop me a line asking if I would like to call to make an appointment to meet him in his Leeds office. His way of contacting me was by way of 'phone calls at 3 a.m. with nobody at the end of the line. You know, silent pressure like the computer driven marketing that we have these days that get you out of the bath just to hear some clicking noises. Mr A. was letting me know they hadn't forgotten. Not to worry - I hadn't forgotten either. Then, one morning, early in May the phone rang as I was dressing for work. I wasn't rushing as the meeting that I intended to be late for was going to be another one of those interminable discussions of protocol and organisation. Some chump had come up with the idea of sending the World Cup – you may recall its real name was the Jules Rimet Trophy – on tour. A chunk of solid gold travelling round England for the masses to gawk at. If they want to see it they should take a look in any newspaper. It's not as if the great unwashed would ever be allowed to touch the damn thing. Anyway the phone rang and I answered it. It was Brian. He spoke nervously.

"Harry. Mr A. wants his two grand."

"Two grand?" says I "It was a thousand a few weeks ago."

"Mr A. is charging you interest of £100 a day. The longer you leave it the more it'll cost you."

"That's daft. I answered. I haven't got two grand today and I won't have two thousand one hundred tomorrow."

"Then you'd better find some way of getting it." He answered "or there'll be a few more things that you won't have tomorrow. Mr A. knows where you are and he's prepared to send some people to visit you. He means it, Harry."

I believed him and I must tell you this news put me somewhat out of sorts. Throughout the morning, when the committee were discussing how the Jules Rimet Trophy could be presented to the nation I found it particularly difficult to concentrate. I had to find a way of getting some serious money very quickly. How could I get two thousand pounds?

And at that moment somebody in the room appeared to have read my mind.

"Two thousand pounds." It was Passmore.

"What?" I bellowed, having been jolted from my thoughts.

"Two thousand pounds. That's how much we have to insure the trophy for. Of course the trophy itself is worth a lot more but the insurance company will only insure the value of the gold. Two thousand pounds." He sat back in his chair smiling.

My mind was racing. "What sort of security measures would we need?" It seemed like a sensible question and Passmore clearly thought so.

"Good question, Harry. We'll have to employ a good security firm to start with and one of us will have to be with the trophy at all times.

It'll mean somebody has to sit with the trophy all day long. Wherever it goes."

Everybody looked at their feet. Nobody was keen to sit, guarding this chunk of precious metal all day long, every day. Especially when they could be enjoying some exciting committees or arranging match security or something similar that involved being very self-important and driving in limousines around London.

The opportunity was handed to me on a plate. I suspect because everybody in the room had realised that I had done practically nothing to help with the organisation of the tournament and that I wouldn't be missed at all.

"How about you?" asked a non-descript official.

"Yes." Seconded Passmore. "Would you like to do it?"

A plan was formulating in my mind but it wouldn't have done to snatch their hands off at this stage. A little bit of reluctance helps. I umm'd and aah'd for a short while and then agreed. I'd take the trophy on a little tour but they must arrange insurance and security. I didn't want anything to go wrong. Motion carried. I had a chance. It was risky but what choice did I have? Mr A. would have sawn one of my legs off. If I was lucky he'd use a sharp saw. If I wasn't it'd be a rusty blade and the only anaesthetic I would have would have been the beating that I'd have been given before they started chopping me up.

Somehow I had to get a message to Mr A. to tell him the plan and to get him to call off the dogs. I also needed an accomplice.

Getting up to Leeds wasn't too difficult. One of the grounds that had been selected as a venue for the World Cup games was Hillsborough in Sheffield. The home of Sheffield Wednesday. I told everybody that some more checks needed to be done on progress and preparation for the World Cup and off to Sheffield I went. All expenses paid and via Leeds. A quick trip to Barnston Snooker Hall put me in touch with

Brian who sent a message to Mr A. to say I wanted a meeting. Within an hour Mr A. and I were chatting in his limousine. I put my plan to him. I would arrange for the Jules Rimet trophy to disappear. It was worth £2,000. Enough to settle my debt with him and all I needed was a few weeks. He gave the matter some thought and decided that he liked the idea and the deal was done. Within two days I was back in London getting ready to take the trophy to a Methodist Chapel in the heart of the London where it was to be displayed to the public. My next problem was to make it disappear without casting any suspicion onto myself.

I checked out the security routine. At the end of each day the trophy was removed from the glass cabinet where it was held and placed in a linen cover then put into a locked container which was chained to my wrist. One of the security guards held the key to the container and the chain so whilst I had the trophy I could never get at it. Overnight the container was locked in a nearby bank safe. I puzzled with how I could extract the trophy from the container or the bank but quickly came to the conclusion that the right answer was for it never to be put into the container. The cover for the trophy was one of those navy blue cloth bags with a string-pull tightener. These were available from Woolworth's, or any other good suppliers to the criminal classes, as they were typically being used by children to hold their plimsolls for school sports. I bought a second bag and folded it into my jacket pocket. As usual I bought a daily newspaper to help me pass the time as I spent my day watching the trophy in its display cabinet. Late in the afternoon of the 20th March I stepped into the toilets and folded my newspaper into the spare bag. I spent a further ten minutes emptying my bowel before I returned, nervously, into the main hall. I hadn't got a case of diarrhoea more a case of total funk. I hid the spare bag under my jacket as it was folded on my arm and with the security guard distracted by the arrival of some members of the public I slipped the spare bag under the display cabinet. So far, so good.

Phase two of the plan was executed when, at the end of the day, the security guard opened the glass cabinet which held the trophy, picked it up and placed it into its navy holder. He pulled the string tight and passed this bag to me. My heart thumped. It was all or nothing now.

"Is the door locked?" I asked him. "Could you check, please?" Over the last couple of days I had made a point of asking the guards to always lock the main doors before taking the trophy out of the cabinet. They understood my concern for security so this guard walked over towards the door to check it was locked. That was my cue to swap the bags over, placing the trophy under the cabinet and putting the second bag into the container, all ready to be put into the bank safe.

Once the container was chained to my arm I realised how much lighter it was than on previous days. Fortunately I would be the only person that would lift the container so nobody else would notice. We delivered it to the bank and I, personally, saw it put under lock and key. Good-night everybody!

Meanwhile back at the Methodist Hall there were no further security worries. There were a few stamps on display that the security guards were worrying about. Something like three million quid's worth. Looking back perhaps we should have picked one up for the ransom note. The main door was left open for worshippers to use and first through the door, after I had left with the container, was my accomplice, Ted. His job was quite simple. It was to walk into the open main hall. Reach under the display cabinet. Pick up the gym bag and take it home. From there I would collect it in due course and, once the deal was done, he could expect his share. I had promised him £100. He could expect it of course but when I'd have it to give him I simply didn't know. My priority was to get Mr A. off my back and to keep the full use of all my limbs.

In case you are interested I had met Ted in a pub in Battersea when I was living in South London. He was an ex-soldier who was a bit down on his luck. I'd bought him a drink and a packet of fags when I had been a bit flush and I knew the temptation of a ton (as he called it) would be enough for him to take on this simple job. He knew very little about me and although he could have picked me out in a line-up I doubted he would. He was an ex-soldier you see. Salt of the earth and somebody you could rely on. I had every intention of paying him, too. It was just a case of first things first. And Mr A. was first on my list of priorities.

All went according to plan. The next morning we collected the container from the bank. Once in the hall I opened the container and as soon as the guard's back was turned pulled out the navy gym bag. The newspaper dropped to the floor. I kicked it under the cabinet where, for all I know, it remains to this day, undiscovered and still with the crossword incomplete. I squealed with anguish. The trophy was gone! Of course a quick search of the room cleared me of any misdeed. The trophy wasn't there. I was outraged at the incompetence of the security team and the bank and everybody else (remember to get your blame in first!) The police were called and I insisted that a full investigation began immediately whilst I returned to FA headquarters to inform the proper authorities.

There was no need for me to let Mr A. know that matters were proceeding according to plan. He only had to listen to the radio or pick up any national or local newspaper and it would tell him all he needed to know except, of course, when I'd be able to deliver the trophy to him. Firstly I needed to collect it from Ted but I wouldn't be able to do that for a few days. I laid low.

Now I know you may be thinking that this was a pretty dastardly thing to do. You know, stealing the World Cup, but think it through for a minute. The Football Association had insured it for £2,000. They would get enough money back to make another one and this time it could be named after an English football person rather than some Frenchman. When did you ever find a Frenchman who knew anything about football?

Then, you say, the Insurance companies are £2,000 down. But hold on! Think of the publicity that the insurance companies are getting out of this. Everybody is reading about the terrible thieves that there are running around and how they are going to steal your trophies if you leave them lying about. So what does Joe Public do? He takes out more insurance policies. For the insurance companies this theft is worth double the £2,000 payout in free advertising alone. It also gives them the opportunity to put up the premiums – but I'm not sure that counts as they were going to find a reason to do that anyway. Think about it – every time there is a major theft the big winners are the insurance companies.

Is that a question from the back? "What about the waste of police time?" Well firstly they <u>love</u> it. A few top law-men get to see their pictures in the paper and their faces on TV. It helps them argue for more coppers on the beat and bigger salaries for themselves and you can bet that they would manage to wangle some free Wembley tickets out of all this.

Now I thought my plan was pretty good. I would get the trophy from Ted and deliver it to Mr A. for him to sell or melt down or whatever he wanted to do but, and this is a lesson for you all when you are pulling your own scams together, the plan changed and that is where things started to go wrong. Mr A. had different ideas, you see. He had realised that the World Cup was worth more to the authorities as a golden trophy than it was to him as a lump of gold. That night, when I arrived home, Brian was loitering outside the entrance to my flat. He nearly made me jump out of my boots when he touched my arm as I used my key to open the door.

"Quick!" He whispered. "Inside." I did move quickly but not quickly enough to get indoors without him following me through the entrance.

Once into my flat Brian explained the change of plan. "Mr A. is going to offer the trophy back to the Football Association for fifteen grand."

Fifteen Grand! Bugger! Why hadn't I thought of that? I could have paid my debts and had a fortune to spare. I suppose that's why Mr A. is where he is - always looking for the bigger deal. You've got to admire people like him.

"Good luck with that." Says I.

"Not quite." Brian corrected my assumption. "Mr A. says a letter will be posted to the FA offering them the deal. Oh Yes!" He added "Have you got an old newspaper and a pair of scissors? I'll need an envelope, some blank paper and some glue too."

I got up to find what I could from his shopping list and he continued.

"We're going to give them forty-eight hours to come up with the cash. Where's the best place for them to give us the money?"

I sat there, stunned. Was he being serious? Did he expect ME to take part in this? I didn't answer him.

"Where is it, anyway?" He was looking around my room.

"Not here of course. It's with a friend near Battersea Park."

"Will that do, then?" He asked. "Shall we do the exchange in Battersea Park?"

I nodded absentmindedly. I was already trying to think of a way out of this. It'd have to be Ted that gave the trophy back. I wasn't going to touch it.

"Yes." I answered "Battersea Park would be fine."

Brian spent the rest of the evening cutting and pasting newspaper onto the blank sheets of paper. I had no glue so he had to use a flour and water mixture. That's another little tip for any of you budding blackmailers out there. Mix a little water with some plain flour and it'll stick paper very nicely. I had picked that idea up myself from watching Blue Peter. Who say's TV is bad for children?

He managed to fold his art-work into an envelope and disappeared before mid-night to post the letter. I was disappointed that he returned shortly afterwards with the intention of sleeping on my floor. Mr A. had paid his rail fare but not given him money for a West End Hotel. Fair point really, they are vastly over-priced.

Blackmail!

Much to my surprise, when I arrived at FA Headquarters the following morning the letter had beaten me to it. You could rely on the Post Office in those days. There was much excitement and no little criticism of Brian's grammar and spelling. Well let's face it, if he had been able to read and write properly he may have been able to get himself a decent job and not be reduced to relying on the grubby business of crime for a living – or football come to think of it. Despite Brian's warning on the letter "Don tell cops or yul not see it agen." the police had been called in. They tut-tutted at the language used in the ransom note and a couple of them, presumably with young children of their own, entered into a deep discussion of how the school system was failing lesser able students. This progressed into a heated debate about how the Labour Party's proposal of Comprehensive Education for all rather than retention of the elite Grammar Schools would (or, as in the opinion of a rather large Police Sergeant, would not) improve standards all round. A few insults were exchanged between the rival factions. One constable was upset at being described as a "Commie Bastard" and was about to strike back in the name of equality when a well-spoken Inspector arrived who trumped all argument by telling the officers that as his kids went to a Public School he didn't give a toss about state education and they should, therefore, "shut the hell up". (He didn't say "hell" but this is meant to be a story for the whole family to enjoy.)

One of the aforementioned members of our elite Police force noticed the tackiness of the ransom letter. "What's this 'orrible glue he's been using? The cuttings are nearly falling off and it smells. This bloke is some kind of idiot."

Now I wouldn't have argued with him about Brian being an idiot but I thought using flour and water to make a paste was a stroke of genius and I felt pretty offended by this great clod's criticism. I bet he'd never tried to organise a theft or blackmailing in his whole life so what right has he to criticise somebody else?

"It's flour and water" I blurted out.

They all looked at me. The Inspector brought the note up to his nose and sniffed it. He then dabbed a wet finger onto a corner of the letter and tasted the paste. "He's right" he said, turning to me with, thank God, a look of admiration and speaking to the other admiring onlookers. "How comes this civvy can work that out and you lot are standing around here talking about kids and politics. You're a bloody shambles the lot of you." They all looked down at their boots. Checking the shine, maybe. "Sergeant Beasley, take this away and get it fingerprinted. He passed over the ransom note. I take it none of you have touched it." He looked at the tops of their heads as they shook them from side to side.

No, I thought, nobody had touched the letter other than me, six FA officials and secretaries, at least three police officers, two journalists who probably both had criminal records, the Inspector himself and a group of representatives from North Korea who had found their way into the boardroom instead of the briefing room on the second floor. If they could find Brian's dabs amongst that lot then fair play to them.

It was very useful for me to be on the inside as the police investigation proceeded. I was pleased that, after due consideration, Mr Mears, who was the man in charge of all the preparations for the World Cup, decided that no risks could be taken. There could be a police presence but the trophy must be retrieved. The "Eyes of the World" were upon us and even the Brazilian authorities were taking the opportunity to poke fun at Britain. Mears would arrange for £15,000 in cash to be made available and, better than that, Mr Mears wanted somebody he could trust to perform the exchange, somebody who would not be tricked by a replica, somebody who was very familiar with the trophy. Yup. You got it. He wanted <u>me</u> to hand over the money. How could I refuse?

That evening I slipped back over to South London and met Ted in a pub, as pre-arranged. I told him of the change of plans. Now Ted was no fool. He knew that the risk of delivering the most famous object in the world right under the noses of the sharpest police force in the world (you have to wonder how bad the rest are, don't you?) and collecting a large sum of cash then walking through Battersea Park with said large sum (and if you don't think <u>that's</u> dangerous – you try it!) was greater than the risk of picking up a package from an unguarded church hall. He wanted a pay rise. They were all at it in those days, the Miners, the Electricity Workers, the M.P.s and now the black-mailer's assistants. We agreed on £500.

Brian was staying in my flat. I wasn't happy about that, not just because he was a slob who didn't clean the bathroom after he had used it and not just because it prevented me from bringing any women home but because I knew he was keeping an eye on me for Mr A. Fifteen thousand pounds was a lot of money. Even for Mr A.

I have pieced together the events of the morning of the exchange from conversations with eye-witnesses who may, or may not, have been telling the truth. Some were reliable whilst others were probably lying through their teeth in order to impress me or to get me to buy them a drink or two. It's terrible the dishonesty of some people, you know.

In a backstreet in Leeds Mr A.'s limousine was packed with muscle in the form of Mr A. himself, Shorty, Mitch and Mike and another heavy who will remain nameless. No disrespect intended I just don't know his name - but if you are reading this, fella, drop me a line and I'll get your name included in the next edition. Can I say fairer than that? In case you are wondering yes, Lurch was at the wheel.

It was a big limo but I reckon even that was crowded with the seven of them in there. By the time they had travelled fifty miles Mike who, with Mitch, had been forced to face backwards had been sick all over Mr A's. expensive Italian shoes. I don't imagine that with the sweat and stink of seven men plus the stench of Mike's vomit that it was a very pleasant journey down to London that morning and, predictably, they were not in a pleasant frame of mind when they eventually arrived in London. If they'd asked me I would have recommended that they stay in Leeds. But they didn't ask.

At Manchester Piccadilly Railway Station the 07:12 pulled out bound for the capital. Sitting in a second class carriage was a grim faced Brennan sporting his traditional donkey-jacket and next to him, fully occupying (and then some) the window seat, sat his daughter, Doreen, dressed in a pink tent. They had eaten breakfast but Doreen took the departure as a signal to open the wrapper of a large pork pie. Her father didn't mind that she had started to eat her packed lunch so early. He wanted her to keep her strength up. They travelled in silence. His first time on an electric train and her first time to London but they were not excited at the thought of their expedition to "The Smoke". This was a business trip.

Another early riser that morning was Mr Robert Steele. Dressed in his smartest black waistcoat and suit he had dusted his bowler hat then picked up his leather brief-case in one hand whilst carrying a small suit-case in the other. The taxi waited to take him from his sub-urban detached house to Leeds Railway Station. At the door his petite wife, still in her dressing gown, pecked her meal-ticket on the cheek and asked him to take care.

"Of course" the slight gentleman replied. "I shall only be a couple of days. Kiss the children for me, dear. I am sorry I shall miss the school end-of-year concerts. I was so looking forward to hearing Jessica play her violin." Even the best of us lie sometimes and Steele was amongst the best of us. He had breezed through his education and qualified as a solicitor at the head of his class and not just because he was a smart as a whip but because he combined that intellect with jolly hard work and a determination to see every job through to a conclusion – and for that reason he was booked in a First Class carriage from Leeds to London with a room at Claridge's awaiting him at the other end. Life was always First Class for Rob Steele, especially when his client could afford it.

The switch was due to take place at 2 p.m. near the boat-lake in Battersea Park. I knew it well. At around 10 a.m. Sergeant Beasley and about a dozen assorted coppers piled into a white Ford Transit van and set off from the car park at the back of West End Central Police Station. Beasley, being the most senior officer, took the front seat next to the driver. The remaining officers squeezed together in the back. Four sat on each side of the van whilst three more squatted on the floor. They all wanted to take part in this operation and under no circumstances would be left out. Each was keen to be the man that caught the fellow who stole the World Cup. As the van moved into Dacre Street they dreamed of their pictures in the newspapers holding the World Cup, prime seats at an England game, a personal thank-you from the Queen, maybe a knighthood or even better – to down a pint or two with Jimmy Greaves. ("My round" says Jimmy. "No. You got the last one. Let me get these." "Hang on. Here comes Mooro. Let him get a round in for a change.") Beasley's chubby cheeks flushed as he delighted in the fantasy.

Doreen Brennan stared out of the window of the train, watching the green countryside of the Midlands fly by. Her father sat silently at her side unblinkingly staring ahead, completely unnerving the man of the cloth sitting opposite him who found him-self repeatedly mouthing "The Lord's Prayer" under his breath.

At a service station on the southbound A1 Mr A. insisted the car was stopped so he could move into the front seat. An argument broke out in the back of the limousine as five heavies vied for the window seats. Mr A. told them all to sit in silence. It all blew up again when Mike pinched Mitch on the inside of his thigh. The others sniggered. Mitch decided to get Mike after school.

Ted wrapped the World Cup in some newspaper and tucked it under his arm. Being a good soldier he had decided to take a good look at the lay of the land and the escape routes, but before he checked the handover spot in Battersea Park he took a detour. When he arrived in the park for this scouting mission he was carrying only a neatly folded Daily Mirror. Ted sat on a park bench and pretended to read the newspaper whilst scanning the area. The missing World Cup trophy was still big news.

I had a lie-in until around 10:30 a.m. and then got up and lazily used the last of the eggs and bread to make scrambled eggs on toast. I had been told to collect the ransom money at the FA Headquarters in Lancaster Gate at one o'clock. So I didn't see much point in rushing around. Brian was still occupying the couch and hadn't moved when I left the flat.

Shortly after I left the flat, at around noon, the door-bell rang. Steele had checked into his hotel then taken a taxi immediately to my address. He was not surprised to be told, by Brian, that I wasn't there and left a message for me to contact him at Claridge's. He then took a taxi to another address in the West End.

Brian tried to settle back on the couch. He had taken to rising late in the afternoon and saw no reason for today to be any different although he was expecting guests later that day. The doorbell rang again. This time a woman's voice asked for me. No doubt curious and in consideration of the female talent which usually turned up at my flat Brian opened the door to take a look. As soon as a crack appeared Brennan put his shoulder to the door and knocked Brian flat onto the floor. Doreen and Brennan let themselves in. Brennan grabbed Brian by the throat and dragged him back into the lounge area. "Where is he?" Brennan asked. Brian did not reply so Brennan shook him in the time-honoured fashion of a rag-doll. But Brian still wasn't talking. Not.

I should add, because he wanted to protect me but because Brennan had him so tightly by the throat that he couldn't speak. Eventually Brian indicated, by pointing at his neck, that he wanted to speak. Brennan loosened his grip and Brian, like a true friend, told him everything that he wanted to know i.e. that I would be at a certain spot in Battersea Park at 2 p.m. Having time to spare Doreen searched the kitchen for food but the cupboards were bare.

"This won't do" says Brennan. "My Doreen needs to keep her strength up."

Brian, advisedly, didn't comment. Doreen was feeling tired after the long journey so Brennan decided to leave for Battersea Park alone but before he did he warned Brian that if he so much as laid a finger on the girl then it'd be broken bones from the neck down. Brian promised to keep his hands to himself. Good decision.

Activity around London continued. Steele set off on a third taxi journey. He didn't tip. This was his client's money he was spending so whilst it was perfectly valid to pay £30 for a night in a top hotel it would be completely inappropriate to give a taxi driver a six-penny tip. Steele had a very clear idea of right and wrong.

The Limo struggled with the traffic as it tried to cross from North to South. Getting across the river has always been a problem. Unless you walk.

I arrived in FA Headquarters and helped to count the £15,000. I was given a small hold-all to carry it in.

The white transit arrived noisily on the edge of the park. The engine was left running and nobody got in or out until, after 10 minutes, the back-doors flew open and two coppers ran into the nearest bushes to take a leak.

Ted had noticed the van's arrival and had been pretending to be reading the last few pages of the newspaper when the doors of the Transit opened. Seeing two uniformed coppers bursting out of the van sent him into an immediate panic. He leapt up and hurtled off as quickly as his thirty-plus-year-old legs would take him.

Beasley, irritated by the commotion at the back of the van got out of the vehicle. He caught sight of Ted running and, with uncharacteristic efficiency, called out to his team "There he is lads, after him!"

The Transit driver slammed his vehicle into gear and set off to prevent the getaway, spilling four of the squad out of the double back doors and onto the road. The leaky coppers buttoned their flies and set off after Ted. The other four jumped up from the asphalt and gave chase. Unfortunately, from where Ted had been sitting, his escape route was severely limited by the lake. He hadn't planned to be making a quick exit until after the exchange. There was a short chase across the grass and flowerbeds until Ted was caught and bundled to the ground by the combined weight of Beasley and one of his men.

From the ground and without forethought Ted denied all knowledge of the Jules Rimet trophy. "I ain't got it! I ain't got it!" He cried.

"You ain't got what?" inquired a future Detective Chief Inspector with urine streaks down the front of his trousers.

Poor Ted was taken straight down to Brixton Police Station where, after handing their charge over to the Desk Sergeant, Beasley and his crew were sent packing by the local constabulary who probably had an eye on a bit of TV coverage and ticket opportunities for themselves. Things nearly got out of hand between the two arms of the Metropolitan Police force until an Inspector turned up to lay claim to Ted. Apparently this inspector had been waiting for a collar like this ever since he had been sent south from Manchester following a very unfortunate drink-driving incident a few years earlier. If he could get Ted to talk then he was on the way back.

Beasley and the gang squeezed back into the Transit and set off into the traffic.

The Big Match

Of course, at the time we at Lancaster Gate knew nothing of all this. We set off around One O'clock to travel across the river. I was taken to the edge of Battersea Park by an FA Official. He patted me on the back, wished me luck and promised there would be a good police presence. I took the hold-all under my arm and started out to find Ted at the agreed place.

Figures got out of a black limousine which was parked a hundred yards further along the road.

Alighting from a London bus nearby a large man in a Donkey Jacket pushed his way through the crowd and strode purposefully across the road heading towards Battersea Park.

Meanwhile I crossed the field, heading for the meeting place. My heart was thumping. The plan, as far as I knew, was on track. I'd hand the cash to Ted, take the trophy and return it to the FA. That would make me even with Mr A. and the world would be a rosy place again. Just like the park, I mused.

If I have eaten cheese or drunk too much port I sometimes wake in the night feeling again the gut-wrenching shock I had when I saw, on the very spot that Ted should have been, none other than Inspector Private School and two beefy coppers. They smiled as they waited for me. I considered running off. I could get a long way with £15,000. South America could be a very friendly place. I turned to check my options but there, following some fifty yards behind me and effectively cutting off my escape was Mike, Mitch and the other fellow (sorry, I still can't remember his name).

My mum would have said that I was caught between the Devil and the Deep Blue Sea and she'd have been about right. I chose the Deep Blue and walked timidly towards the Inspector.

"Mr Barker" he called as I approached. "I am glad we caught you."

I bet you are, I thought.

"We've got some good news." He smiled. "We've got the fellow that took the World Cup."

He's toying with me, thinks I.

"Yes. It's a fellow we were keeping an eye on. I had a clue that it was him and was just waiting for him to make a mistake. Oh Yes." He chuckled proudly as he lied. "It was just a matter of time."

Of course he hadn't had a clue all along but I wasn't going to argue. I assumed they had picked Ted up and by the Inspector's manner I'd say Ted hadn't grassed on me. I never thought he would, you see. It's that thing about being in the Army – honour and all that. I reckoned I could rely on Ted. I breathed a sigh of relief and wiped a drop of sweat from my brow.

"Now then" said the Inspector, with a satisfied grin that only a copper who is anticipating a good collar and the possibility of promotion could give. "You'd better let me and these two fine Constables take that hold-all full of cash. You don't want to be walking around here with that sort of money. We'll take it to the F.A. for you. Could we give you a lift back?" I wasn't sure about getting into a Police Car. "We've got to pop into Brixton Nick on the way, though. I want to have a chat with the fellow we picked up this morning. Maybe you'd like to take a look at him?"

I didn't want to take a look at him. I already knew very well what he looked like. But, as it happened I was quite happy to walk to the waiting police car with the Inspector and his two fine chums; especially as doing so meant walking right past the three stooges who, on seeing me engaged in conversation with these fine officers of the law, had become engrossed in the flora which was on display in the park. As I strolled past they showed particular interest in some budding dahlia thus shielding their faces from the Inspector. Wise fellows.

I stayed with the policemen until they reached their car at the corner of Prince of Wales Drive and MacDuff Road. I then thanked them warmly and set off along MacDuff Road as quickly as I could, resisting the desire to burst into a run. The police car sped off, its bell ringing in alarm to indicate that either there was a murder to prevent or a warm lunch which needed to be eaten before it cooled. A quick look over my shoulder confirmed that not only had the three followed me but that they had been joined by the limousine holding Mr A., Shorty and Lurch. As my head turned and I broke into a trot I suddenly found myself on the floor. I had walked into a brick wall. The brick wall bent over and brought me to my feet. It was Brennan. I would say that he held my arm in a vice-like grip but I don't think I have ever managed to tighten a vice that much.

I looked back and at the end of the street. Mr A. was standing at the door of his vehicle. The others had spread across the width of the road and were approaching Brennan and me.

I would like to say that they were five of the ugliest thugs that I had ever seen in my life but that wouldn't have given due credit to the fellow second from the left (the one whose name I can't remember) who had clearly put a lot of effort into his appearance. His chiselled jaw would no doubt have served him well with the ladies in whatever seedy dive he chose to spend his evenings and he wore one of those collarless Beatle jackets the cut of which was only spoiled by the thick, steel knuckle-duster that he drew from an inside pocket and placed in his left hand.

A quick look over my shoulder showed me an opportunity to escape and I would have taken it were it not for Brennan's grip on my arm.

"Hang on, lad" said Brennan. Clearly recognising my pursuers and understanding my, and their, intent. "We can take 'em".

"Or," I replied "we could run away!"

"There's just five of 'em." Brennan answered.

"Yes. That's why we should run away."

"They're not as tough as they look." He argued.

"That's right. We've got nothing to prove." I suggested.

"They are more scared of us than we are of them."

This conversation had turned into "The Battle of the Common Phrase or Saying" and Brennan had won. He was clearly right on this last count because whilst we had turned up like a pair of Gentlemen Jims with nothing to protect ourselves but our upright stance, our bare fists and an honourable sense of right and wrong Mr A.'s henchmen had taken the cowardly precaution of bringing the aforementioned knuckle-duster, a bike chain, a pen-knife with one of those things for getting stones out of horses hooves (although I wasn't sure how Lurch was going to use that until he put the body of the knife in his palm and closed his fist to show the pointy-bit protruding between his middle fingers - I wondered what kind of sick mind would think of using a good scouting tool in such a depraved way.) Also there was the baseball bat (you didn't see many of them in those days so presumably Shorty had holidayed recently in the States. I didn't ask) and lastly a piece of metal about two foot long that looked like a blade from one of those Hover-Mowers. Hover-Mowers hadn't been invented then so I could only assume it was an inappropriately shaped piece of scrap metal. That'd be pretty sore on his hands I should think. I bet he goes for a baseball bat next time, I thought. I mean – look at the way that little fellow is swinging that bat about. I bet he could crush a rock with that!

I had an idea. I whispered to Brennan. "We can't beat them all but one on one we'd have a chance!"

"Brave lad." He replied "But I am not going to let you do this on your own."

He'd got it completely wrong. I didn't mean ME one on one, I meant for him to take them on one at a time but he'd given me an opening. "Alright then. You do it. I don't mind." I called out "OK fellas. Let's do this fairly. He'll take you on one at a time. Who's first?"

They paused their forward movement to glance at each other. A small grin spread through the group like a contagious virus afflicting each of their faces in turn. Then Lurch, the evil Boy-Scout, answered with a snigger. "All of us." I definitely didn't like that fellow. They stepped forward again. The Beatle (I have to give him a name) had found a second knuckle-duster for his right hand. An interesting thought for you, perhaps out of context of the story at this time but none-the-less valid for all that, is that people complain about footballers not being able to kick equally well with both feet but nobody complains that boxers don't punch as well with both hands. Food for thought that, and something you might want to talk about in the pub later. But not, I suggest, with an easily offended pugilist!

As they approached us Brennan remained still and held my arm tightly. His eyes never left the approaching group as he spoke to me using the corner of his mouth. A muted whisper. "I want to have a word with you" he began as if we were a couple of old friends about to enjoy a mixed social and business engagement. "My Doreen is in the family way."

At that moment I thought Shorty may have caught me round the back of the head with the baseball bat. I looked again but Shorty was still ten yards away, the mob had begun to circle Brennan and me. No. Something else had felt like a hammer-blow to my skull.

"I've come to make sure you do the decent thing." Brennan was presumably speaking English as a foreign language. Although I knew the words he was using I didn't understand them in this context. I looked at him. He was serious. He glanced at me briefly raising his eyebrows in a questioning manner. His grip hadn't loosened. "You are going to do the decent thing, aren't you?" I hadn't met a refugee from the planet "Fair-Play" for a few years but it appeared that Brennan was just such an alien.

Now, if I were to tell you that I stood back and looked Brennan in the eye, raised myself to my full height, shook his hand and promised him that I'd do the right thing by his daughter and that father and future son-in-law then set about thrashing the bullies that had surrounded us and sent them packing you would, of course, be quite right to call me a bloody liar. But it ain't that far from the truth.

Of course I told Brennan I'd do the right thing and that made him happy. What else could I say and what point would there be in saying anything else? Once this lot had finished with me the only Church service I'd be attending would be my own funeral. Still, he trusted me so he let go of my arm. It was too late by then for me to make my escape. The boys from Leeds had surrounded us and were closing in, their weapons at the ready. Lurch with a metal spike protruding from his massive knuckles. Shorty swinging the baseball bat. Mitch (not the sharpest fellow amongst a pretty dull bunch) had the misshapen metal thing. Mike was swinging the bike chain at his side like a lethal skipping rope. The fifth man, the Beatle, was shaping up nicely with his hands in front of his body, his shoulders rounded like a professional boxer with his knuckledusters at the ready.

"We haven't got the money." I cried "You just saw that copper take it off me!"

Lurch, the self-appointed leader, replied "Mr A. wants his money."

Negotiations were at an end. It was hardly Yalta but there was nothing more to say. They wanted the money and I simply didn't have it. There are times in a man's life when he has to decide whether to run or to stand and fight. There are other times when the decision is made for him because some great gorilla has grabbed hold of his arm.

All credit to Brennan though. He immediately saw the danger man on the opposition side and dealt with him. He charged towards Lurch and with the swiftest of movements landed a massive blow into Lurch's unprotected belly. All six foot seven of Lurch was lifted from the ground as Brennan's fist disappeared into his stomach. Lurch toppled and fell like a mighty redwood which had been scythed at its base. Unfortunately, while Brennan had taken out Lurch, Shorty had taken the opportunity to land a solid blow from the baseball bat across his unprotected back. It knocked Brennan off balance and gave an opportunity for the Beatle and Mike to lay into him with their weapons. Needless to say this breaking of ranks by the opposition had given me the opportunity to slip between the defenders and, having seen an opportunity to get away, I was going to take it. Unfortunately, Mitch dropped the metal object that he was carrying and leapt after me catching my legs at the waist and bringing me to the ground. I suspected he had gone to a school that played rugby rather than football. It wasn't a tackle that one would have expected to see in the professional football leagues although I did see something similar tried on George Best a few times.

I managed to grab Mitch around his head and held it securely against my chest. I wrapped my legs around his body and held on as tight as I could. The theory being that he couldn't hurt me whilst I held on to him. I was wrong. The bastard, with his head against my chest, bit me hard around my right nipple. I could show you the scar today. It was agonising so (and I assure you this was purely in retaliation and not, as has been suggested because I was a sissy) I screamed so loudly that I believe I perforated his eardrum.

Brennan was putting up a great fight against the other thugs. Shorty's nose was pouring blood and he appeared dazed. I believe it was broken. Brennan had taken possession of the chain and was using it to great effect on Lurch – who had returned to the fray. The baseball bat had been discarded and lay on the floor next to Mike who was holding one of his hands in the other. Presumably he had hit Brennan so hard with his fist that it had broken. The Beatle was pummelling Brennan's back to little effect but it was obvious that Brennan couldn't last much longer. As I held Mitch close I saw Shorty pick up, and swing, the baseball bat. It connected with Brennan just below the knee and he started to fall to the ground.

Where, the taxpayers of South London may ask, were Britain's Finest at this time?

Having left Brixton in disappointment Sergeant Beasley and his comrades had decided to return to their station. Beasley couldn't believe his eyes as they turned a corner in their white van. There, in the middle of the road, was a scene straight out of the Seven Samurai except we were fighting amongst ourselves, of course. Under the Sergeant's orders the van accelerated towards the fray and the doors were thrown open. The policemen were in a particularly foul mood having had they prey stolen by the Brixton Nick and, as the football season had ended a few weeks ago, there had been no recent opportunities to clobber some "hooligans". They were fully charged and ready for action. Out they piled from their wagon and laid into all around them. I took a couple of blows myself until Sergeant Beasley recognised me. Had they been organised they would have been able to arrest the Leeds gang but they were not interested in that. They just wanted to take out their frustration on somebody and this was an ideal opportunity. The Leeds hoodlums took their chance and legged-it up the street to jump into the limousine. While the coppers slapped each other on the back and bragged of their exploits Lurch chucked the vehicle into reverse and swung it around heading off back across the river towards North London. Brennan was lying in the road. A bone in his leg had been broken by the blow from the baseball bat but he still attempted to stand. I quickly explained to Sergeant Beasley that the other fellows had tried to mug me whilst Brennan had stepped in to help. I promised him that I would come to the station later to make a statement and he called for an ambulance to take Brennan to hospital.

Other than the nasty bite on my chest I had managed to suffer just a few bruises. The policemen had done more damage to me than Mr A's boys but I couldn't complain – mind you nobody would have cared if I had. I left before the ambulance arrived to take Brennan away but not before he had reminded me of my promise (you remember – to do the "right thing") and told me that Doreen was at my home. He expected me to go straight back there to see her. I said I would, well I needed a change of clothes anyway.

I should have realised something was wrong when I saw some drops of blood outside the front door of my flat. Now you would have thought that having taken a bit of a beating at the hands of Brennan and the Law Mr A. and friends would have set off immediately for the safety of their own home town. And that's what I thought but not so these tough Yorkshire-men. Whilst his henchmen had taken a bit of a thrashing Mr A. was untouched and still keen to get his money. He saw me as the key to doing that and he and his team had made their way back to my flat where Brian had opened the door to let them in.

Doreen sat on my bed. She beamed a huge smile at me when I stepped through the door. Her hero had come to rescue her.

"Harry. You came!" I think she expected me to rush forward into her arms. As it happens I did rush forward but only because Lurch had grabbed my arm and pulled me into the room closing the door behind me.

Mr A. was sitting on the couch. He had thrown the spare bed-linen onto the floor. Who's going to pick that up? I thought.

"Come in, Harry." He waved me forward. "Sit with me."

I stepped forward and placed myself at the far end of the couch.

"That was very impressive earlier, Harry. You and that big fellow put up a good fight. Where is he?" there was a slight nervousness in his voice. He clearly wouldn't want to meet Brennan again.

"He's fine." I answered "I am expecting him any minute."

"That's strange" Interrupted Mike. We heard on the radio that one of the fellows involved in a fight in Battersea was in hospital. I take it that isn't you?" The whole world loves a comedian. The other Yorkshire-men allowed themselves another menacing chuckle.

Mitch asked "Have you got any food in this flat?"

"No. Sorry. I had the last of the eggs and bread this morning." I was glad that I'd finished them off. If this lot are going to kill me in my flat they'll have to do it on an empty stomach. "Shall I go to the shop and get something?" I asked, hopefully.

"Ooh, yes." Doreen joined in. All concern forgotten at the thought of a good meal. "I'm hungry and Dad says I must keep my strength up."

We all looked at each other and one or two smiled. Not me though, especially when Doreen added. "I'm having Harry's baby so I have to eat well."

They all looked at me with a mixture of sympathy and contempt except Mitch who piped up "Congratulations!" and slapped me on the back.

Mr A. glared at me, his eyes narrowing in threat. "I hope you are going to do the decent thing." It really was a question which needed the right reply otherwise I could see some very real bodily damage coming my way.

"Of course I will" and then to add conviction in the face of Mr A.'s apparent disbelief. "I love her."

I didn't blink and he believed me, I think, and from the giggles coming from the direction of the bed, I'd say simpering Doreen did too.

Mike was sent out to get some food whilst Mr A. and I discussed ways in which I could help compensate him and his gorillas for his investment and their injuries. Mr A. was very aware that whilst there had been much in the news about the arrest of the man who had stolen the World Cup no mention had been made of the World Cup itself being found. It therefore followed that somebody still had the World Cup which was worth in the region of £15,000 to him. And the "somebody" that he believed <u>had</u> the World Cup was none other than yours truly. I explained that only Ted knew where it was and that Ted was locked up in Brixton awaiting Her Majesty's pleasure. Mitch's idea was that I should go to Brixton and find out from Ted where the trophy was. The problem, as I explained to the gathered company, was that Ted would tell nobody other than me where it was hidden but if I were to go to the jail and ask him then I'd quickly end up in there with him.

We mulled things over for a while and then Mr A. sent Mike out to do some more shopping. Mike wasn't too happy about running another errand for Mr A. but a few sharp words from "The Boss" kept him in line. That's another pointer for any of you who are planning to set yourself up as a gangland leader, you have to be prepared to crack the whip now and then to keep your henchmen in order. Mr A.'s method of choice was to use a hard stare, a deep growl and a few barked orders. That's how he remained "top dog" I suppose.

The next morning, the 27th April 1966, an extremely tall woman wearing a large pink dress left my flat and boarded a bus to cross the river. Once there this woman made her way to Brixton jail and asked to speak to a prisoner there. The man had been arrested the day before under suspicion of theft. Police had been questioning him throughout the evening but to no avail. An inspector was due to arrive shortly to continue the investigation.

The arrested man and the tall, plain woman spoke for ten minutes. Observers were surprised to see them shake hands at the end of the conversation. A police officer followed the woman as she left the jail. They tracked her for half an hour until she disappeared into a public lavatory in Clapham station. The woman was never seen again however when the toilets were thoroughly searched a wig, a pair of size 12 ladies shoes and a pink dress smeared with lipstick and mascara were found in one of the cisterns.

At another flat in London a Mr Steele arrived and asked to speak to the residents. They asked how he had come to contact them and he explained that he had traced the individual through employment and tax records. It was elementary, he explained. They were, however, unable to help him but he left his business card and asked to be contacted at Claridge's should any further information become available. Harvey confirmed he would be pleased to help if at all he could.

Whilst I had been visiting Ted in Brixton prison Mike had taken a change of my clothes and a pair of my shoes to Clapham Station. It was easy to give the police the slip as they were looking for a very tall woman and by the time I had come out of the toilet I had become a tall, young man. I had some difficulty removing the make-up and had used Doreen's dress to wipe away what I could. Mr A. had insisted that Mike stayed with me as I collected the trophy from where Ted had hidden it. This was despite my assertion that I would have to come back to the flat for the woman that I loved – thinking back I may have over-cooked that just a little bit.

I am here to tell you that if Ted hadn't described to me exactly where the trophy was hidden it would never have been found. As you no doubt know the Jules Rimet Trophy, interchangeable known as the World Cup, was about 14 inches (35cm) high and made of solid gold. The thing about gold is that it don't rust. So where else would you hide it other than under water? In Clapham Common, close to Battersea Park, there was a large pond. There were areas around it where the over-hanging trees gave plenty of cover and Ted had placed the trophy, wrapped in an old newspaper, in the mud at the edge of the pond. It took me about 10 minutes of groping around in the sludge and dead vegetation to find the trophy and to lift it to the surface. As I pulled the weighty lump from the murky water Mike latched on to it and tried to snatch it from me. Clearly he had plans of his own. Perhaps he was fed up of running to and from the shops at Mr A.'s behest and fancied the idea of setting up on his own. He was trying to steal the trophy from its rightful owner, me! After all I had been through I was not about to let my treasure go so held on to it as best I could. As we wrestled in the filthy sludge I noticed that we were being watched by a curious black and white mongrel. Its head held to one side and an ear cocked as if it couldn't believe its eyes.

Mike managed to take possession of the trophy but as he stood up to make his escape I managed to grab his ankle. He slipped on a particularly soft patch of mud and fell to the ground in front of me, dropping his prize. In a flash I picked it up and fetched Mike a well-deserved wallop across the back of his head. I then lit out of there as if my life depended on it - which it did.

By the time Mike was back on his feet I was out of sight and moving. Nothing was going to catch me. Nothing that is, except that small black and white mongrel dog who had taken up the chase. It was barking as if it was important that the whole world knew about the running man. I turned momentarily to take a look at the animal. I knew that dog and the dog knew me. It caught the turn-up in my trouser-leg in its teeth and tried to slow me down. I kicked out with my leg and sent him spinning away, his short claws scrabbling to grip the asphalt path. I ran off but he was back up and after me again. In the distance I could see Mike who, no doubt had been attracted by the incessant barking, was running towards me. We left Clapham Common and trailed westward. Me, the dog and, a fair way behind, Mike. I found myself heading back towards Clapham Station. I didn't want to go back there in case the police were still around so turned southward to head towards Battersea. The dog continued to give chase so I turned, once again, eastward, sprinting as best I could through the back-streets, trying to get some distance between me and my followers. The dog seemed to be enjoying himself and continued to bark and yelp happily, attracting the attention of every household in the region.

Now I kept myself pretty fit in those days and I realised that Mike was no match for me when it came to a sprint. The pesky mutt, however, I could not shake off. Having run around a mile at full pace through the streets of London and with all the exertions of the previous day, not to mention the weight of the trophy, I found myself tiring and slowing down. People had been staring at the big man being chased by the little dog and some children had broken into fits of laughter at the sight. I could hardly go another step. I slowed to a walk, then, noting there were few people about and seeing an opportunity I surreptitiously slipped the trophy out from under my jacket and into a thick, deep hedge. I walked briskly away. If anybody had stopped me then they wouldn't have found the trophy and I could come back for it later but where was that pesky dog now?

I walked a further twenty yards and turned to look back. The dog had stopped at the very spot where I had stashed the trophy. His curiosity had got the better of him and he had decided to stay rather than to continue the chase. A man arrived calling out for "Pickles". The dog responded and directed his owner to the hidden loot. I turned and quickly walked away. I had tried but could do no more. The game was up. I needed somewhere to lie low. I could only think of one place.

A friend in need is a friend indeed and I was indeed in need. I had just about ten bob in my pocket and could not go back to my own flat without the trophy or the money to pay Mr A. so I knocked apologetically at Harvey's door. I hadn't seen either Harvey or Robert for some time but I was confident that all our problems were behind us. They both greeted me warmly and pushed a glass of fashionable wine into my hand. I have never been particularly fond of wine but it was the thought that counted. I took a shower and whilst I did Harvey took it upon himself to call Claridge's. Robert did what he could to clean my mud-splattered clothes. By the time I had dried and wrapped myself in a towel the taxi had pulled up and Steele had arrived at the door. There were no clothes in my size in the flat. Everything that Harvey and Robert wore was very tight on them. On me it would be obscene. Seeing the suited toff at the door I grabbed one of Harvey's lilac shirts and pulled it on. I managed to button it at my waist but my hairy chest remained uncovered.

As Steele entered the room Robert was complaining that I had smeared the black mascara onto one of his best towels.

Exhausted and exasperated I sat on the sofa between Robert and Harvey, sipping the wine, and listened to what Mr Steele had to say. "Your mother's will" he explained "left everything to you."

Fine, I thought, that means nothing. But then Steele explained further.

"A certain Charles Harold Mulligan of Wisconsin, Ohio also departed this mortal coil some three months ago. It seems that during the last war Mr Mulligan, a famous sportsman, had grown attached to your mother and, having no heir himself and some regrets in that direction, left his not inconsiderable fortune to her. Some $20,000,000 US Dollars in cash plus controlling interest in several sporting ventures including a chain of fifty sports shops across several of the United States. This property therefore forms part of the maternal estate and subsequently falls to you, sir. Minus, of course, reasonable expenses such as those covering the extensive work that Steele, Hyde and Hope have performed in tracing you. There are, however, certain conditions. One, quite strange, is that if you father a child outside a loving marital relationship then the whole of the fortune will pass to an orphanage in America run by the Unorthodox Church of the Reformed Fornicator."

He looked at me with the stained towel around my waist and with Harvey and Robert either side of me like bookends, and said "as the Executor of this Will I have to ask - it is likely that you would ever father a child... outside a loving marital relationship?"

I looked him straight in the eye, one hand fell onto Harvey's knee, and I answered "Not a bleeding chance!".

At this point Harry smiled contentedly at the memory and closed his eyes. He appeared to gently drop off to sleep. The biographer considered the option of waking him to continue his story however, when Harry abruptly and audibly passed wind the biographer, along with the staff and other guests at the Football Association's Headquarters, took the option to leave the room, quickly! There would always be another day!

Background to the Story.

Garrincha

Garrincha was born in 1933 in a small town called Pau Grande. Amazingly, for such a gifted sportsman, he was born with 'bent' legs - his left bent out and his right bent in. When young, he was also smaller than the kids his own age and was christened 'garrincha' (the local name for a 'little bird') by his sister.

He played for Brazil 60 times, winning the World Cup twice; he dismantled and demoralised the highly-rated USSR team in the 1958 Finals and, some say, won the tournament nearly single-handedly in 1962.

Garrincha's life was also hugely colourful off the pitch. He was, allegedly, very well endowed, which may help explain why he was so popular with the ladies. He fathered (at least) 14 children by 5 different women, including eight daughters with his first wife, Nair, and a son in Sweden - conceived while on tour with Botafogo. It seems he was anything other than a devoted husband to Nair. Throughout his marriage to her, he regularly chased other women - he had a number of girlfriends and one-night stands and had children with several of them.

Only one woman came close to 'taming' him: Elza Soares, a well-known singing star and every Brazilian man's fantasy. The pair met in 1961 and began their affair the following year. However, the public were less than impressed when news of their relationship broke, something that caused a great deal of trouble for them.

Garrincha also suffered from alcoholism - cachaça, made from fermented sugar cane, was a particular favourite - and it was this affliction that led to his death at the age of 49.

How Pickles the dog dug up the accursed World Cup

Taken from the story told by Paul Fleckney

The trophy was audaciously pinched on March 20 1966 from under the noses of the footballing authorities, who were proudly exhibiting it in the Methodist Central Hall, Westminster, prior to England's hosting of the tournament.

Edward Bletchley, a 46-year-old former soldier, was accused of the theft (although he claimed to be merely a middle man, receiving £500 for his troubles) and was thought to be responsible for attempting to blackmail Joe Mears, then chairman of the FA and Chelsea Football Club, into paying a £15,000 ransom for the return of the nine-inch solid gold statue.

Mears agreed to the deal, which was to be performed at a clandestine rendezvous with Bletchley in Battersea Park, but ignored his demand for the police to remain oblivious.

In the run-up to the exchange Bletchley became suspicious of a transit van, which he correctly guessed to be a police back-up team, and fled. The attempt ended in his arrest and Bletchley shortly found himself in Brixton prison.

With the finals looming and the world's eyes on England to deliver a competition to remember, the cup was still missing.

The details from this point are sketchy but it is believed that, from his cell, Bletchley struck another deal with the police. He wanted a lady friend to visit him in prison and, if they obliged without interfering, the trophy would materialise.

Days later the cup was in Pickles' paws.

Pickles the dog ferreted out the stolen Jules Rimet World Cup trophy in his Norwood garden.

The short version of events is that the dog's owner went across the road to make a call from a public telephone box when Pickles spied a parcel in his front garden and dragged him over.

Sadly, some time later, Pickles choked to death when his lead snagged on a fallen tree during a cat chase

Leeds United.

A major football team based in the North of England. They enjoyed enormous success under manager Don Revie around 1970.

Moustachioed Harry is on the back row to the right of the goalkeeper.

The write up of this history
http://www.mightyleeds.co.uk/seasons/196162.htm

agrees with some of Harry's version of events.

Nobby Stiles

Norbert "Nobby" Peter Stiles MBE was the front- toothless midfield ball-winner of England's 1966 World Cup winning side. He made his debut for Manchester United against Blackburn Rovers in 1960.

George Best

George Best played for Manchester United between 1963 and 1973 and brought great success to that club. He is considered by many to be one of the world's best-ever footballers but his popularity transcended football as he became a fashion icon attracting the attention of many of the world's most desirable women. George suffered from alcoholism which after a lengthy struggle proved to be his downfall. If George wasn't the best footballer the world has ever seen, and he may have been, he was certainly the most exciting.

Bobby & Jack Charlton

Bobby, the younger brother, played for Manchester United and became recognised internationally as one of the greatest players of his era whilst Jackie, a Leeds player and also a World Cup winner made an enormous contribution to football in Ireland through his management of their national team.

James William Thomas "Jimmy" Hill OBE

Jimmy Hill is the only person in the history of football to have been player, coach, manager, director and chairman of a Football League Club. He is also a qualified referee and as an emergency measure he once took the role of linesman for a league game at Highbury. In 1957, he became chairman of the Professional Footballers Association and campaigned to have the Football League's £20 maximum wage scrapped, which he achieved in January 1961.

Between 1961 and 1966, as manager, he took Coventry City from the Third to the First division. In 1968 he became Head of Sport at London Weekend Television and rose to Deputy Controller of Programmes, before joining the BBC as presenter of "Match of the Day" for which he is probably most famous.

If you think Harry Barker's story is unbelievable then read the story of Jimmy Hill's life and think again!

Bradford Park Avenue

Bradford Association Football Club (almost always referred to as 'Park Avenue') is a football club based in Bradford, West Yorkshire, England. The club's name comes from its old stadium at Park Avenue in Bradford. They were placed in the Fourth Division after the league reorganisation in 1958 and although they won promotion to the Third Division in 1961, they were relegated back to the Fourth Division in 1963. After several seasons of struggle, they were voted out of the Football League in 1970 and went into liquidation in 1974.

The margin between success and failure in football can often be measured in inches. For Park Avenue the few points lost, possibly as the result of Harry's intervention, may have made the difference between failing to survive and growing into a major football club. We will never know!

John Perfumo

Perfumo was a British soldier, politician, and charity worker. He was the central character in what has become known as the "Profumo Affair" which remains one of Britain's most infamous sex scandals. In 1960 he became secretary of state for war in the Conservative cabinet. Profumo was handsome, wealthy and a personal friend of Queen Elizabeth II. He was married to Valerie Hobson, an actress, but in 1963 stories began to circulate that whilst in office he had an affair with a prostitute, Christine Keeler. If that wasn't bad enough it transpired that Keeler had also been involved with a certain Yevgeny Ivanov, who was the Soviet military attaché in London.

At first Profumo denied the stories but later, having lied to Parliament, admitted that they were true. He was forced to resign in June from both the cabinet and Parliament. The scandal contributed to the fall of Macmillan's British government in October 1963.

Stephen

Possibly this is Dr. Stephen Thomas Ward who was one of the central figures in the 1963 Profumo affair. Ward introduced the married British cabinet minister and MP John Profumo to Christine Keeler at a house party hosted at Lord Astor's country home, Cliveden, in the summer of 1961.

However it is rumoured that Profumo had already been introduced to Keeler by Ward in a club called Murray's the previous evening. Harry may have witnessed this event.

Benny Hill

Alfred Hawthorne "Benny" Hill was an English comedian, actor and singer, notable for his long-running television programme The Benny Hill Show. Despite enormous popularity he, and his shows, which often included what some people would consider smutty innuendo as well as scantily clad women, were eventually driven from the TV screens. A comic genius.

Mary Quant

Mary Quant is an iconic British fashion designer, one of the many designers who took credit for inventing the miniskirt and hot pants. In November 1955, she teamed up with her husband, Alexander Plunkett-Greene to open a fashion shop. The miniskirt, for which she is arguably most famous, became one of the defining fashions of the 1960s. Quant's popularity was at its height in the mid 1960s, during which time she produced the dangerously short micro-mini skirt.

Jerome and Jim

Possibly Harry is referring to the two young actors, Gerome Ragni and James Rado, who created the musical HAIR for the New York stage.

HAIR was conceived and brought together by them over a three-year period, 1964 - 1967. The musical celebrates their pacifist Bohemian lifestyle, vehemently condemns the Vietnam War, and embraces the sexual revolution. This rock musical is probably most famous for the complete nudity of the actors and actresses.